D1468248

Entrepreneurship and Innovation:
Global Insights from 24 Leaders

Edited by James C. Barrood

ROTHMAN INSTITUTE
OF ENTREPRENEURSHIP

SILBERMAN COLLEGE OF BUSINESS
FAIRLEIGH DICKINSON UNIVERSITY

Copyright © 2010
Rothman Institute of Entrepreneurship

Editor: James C. Barrood
Copy Editor: Brian Moran
Production & Design: Mahesh Nair

Rothman Institute of Entrepreneurship
Silberman College of Business
Fairleigh Dickinson University

Contents

INTRODUCTION

As the head of the Rothman Institute of Entrepreneurship at Fairleigh Dickinson University's Silberman College of Business, I am delighted to share this publication. It is designed to help students, entrepreneurs and innovators as they pursue their ventures, initiatives and dreams. Over the past 21 years, we have hosted some of the world's foremost thinkers and practitioners in the areas of entrepreneurship and innovation. This book highlights excerpts of their excellent talks.

I hope this will be your go to book - one you refer to again and again when you need to hear the voices of experience discuss their lessons learned, best practices and inspirations. The collective wisdom found in these pages is as impressive as it is honest. We thank our world-class contributors - innovators and entrepreneurs - who were willing to share their personal stories.

The mission of the Rothman Institute is to educate, inspire and support entrepreneurs and innovators in the academic, business and nonprofit communities. In compiling the best speeches given at our events, we hope this book reinforces our mission statement for years to come.

We are thankful for the hard work and dedication that has been a hallmark of our organization. We thank the former staff and faculty as well as our current "family" who have served passionately to create one of the finest entrepreneurship centers in the world. It has been a wonderful journey since our founding in 1989, and we look forward to many more years of nurturing success locally, nationally and globally.

The global leaders highlighted in this book have participated in our leading programs over the past two decades, and most of their presentations have been videotaped. While the vignettes are edited versions of their speeches and interviews, their full-length talks can be easily accessed online. Send an e-mail to rothman@fdu.edu with "Insights" in the subject line and we will connect you to all of the videos.

James C. Barrood
Executive Director
Rothman Institute of Entrepreneurship, www.fdu.edu/rothman

CHAPTER 1

Innovative Leadership in Growing Companies

An interview with John Bailye, executive chairman of EKR Therapeutics, and founder and former chairman and CEO of Dendrite International

John Bailye

John Bailye sat down to talk with James Barrood about his entrepreneurial experience in spring 2008 as part of the "Voices of Innovation" television series. At the time, he had recently stepped down as the founder, chairman and CEO of Dendrite International Inc. after it was bought in 2007 by Cegedim, a French multinational.

In 1986, Bailye established Dendrite International Inc. to pioneer the development of software applications for pharmaceutical sales-force management. Originally based in Bailye's native Australia, Dendrite relocated to New Jersey in 1987.

In 2005, *Forbes* magazine listed Dendrite among the 200 best small companies, and Dendrite ranked No. 61 on *Business 2.0's* "100 Fastest Growing Technology Companies." In 2000, *Fortune* magazine listed Dendrite 44 among the 100 fastest-growing companies in the United States.

As of spring 2010, Bailye is executive chairman of EKR Therapeutics Inc., a privately held specialty pharmaceutical company focused on providing critical-care products for the hospital setting.

James Barrood: John, as the founder and former CEO of Dendrite International, you came to this country 21 years ago with a new, innovative venture that had $175,000 in sales. Last year, that same company had over $400 million in sales when it was sold. John, tell us what innovation means to you.

> **John Bailye:** To me, innovation is all about understanding a current problem and then finding a new solution. Some companies, such as Google, have become innovative by inventing a problem, defining the solution and then inventing products to solve it. At Dendrite, we were not that smart. We saw a big problem and figured out that a solution wasn't going to be found in the traditional ways that companies were doing it. We had to go in a different direction. This is how we define innovative leadership.

Barrood: How did you maintain innovative leadership at Dendrite over the years?

> **Bailye:** In terms of innovative leadership, I think most founding CEOs have a healthy dose of fear. I imagine them looking in the mirror on a daily basis and wondering if they are still the right person to run the company. Andy Grove once said, "Only the paranoid survive." I believe he was half right. In order to be successful, CEOs need to be truly fearful that they might not be good enough for the position. It's a very different job running a $200 million company versus running a $2 million company. In a $2 million company, you know everyone and everyone knows you. Employees and customers have access to you, your vision and your time. In a $200 million company, it's more complicated to deliver your message and your vision. It's harder to keep everyone on the same page.

At the same time, when I talk to entrepreneurs and people running growing companies, my message to them is to trust themselves more. It is quite difficult to successfully grow an entrepreneurial company. The anecdotal history is that most entrepreneurs and leaders aren't successful; the growing company spits them out somewhere along the line. But, if you have somehow survived the growing pains, my message is to be more confident in your own decision-making. To the degree that innovation needs to have a central location, it should reside with the company leader. Their ability to stay in touch with customers and to be confident decision makers will be the biggest driver of innovation.

A separate, but related, issue is whether a growing company continues to be innovative. One of my advantages as CEO of Dendrite was not having a technology background. I had no intellectual commitment to any of our platforms. My commitment was to outperform our competition, and to solve the bigger problems of our customers. If that meant destroying a pre-existing product in order to meet those goals, it wasn't a difficult decision for me because I had no technological basis for being wedded to the earlier products.

At some point in the lifecycle of every product the company will want to commercialize it. Innovation can sometimes get in the way of profit maximization. Of the many businesses we acquired over the years, most had too many products that diverted the company's scarce resources. The companies had opportunities, but they lacked the proper management team to take advantage of those opportunities. In a perfect world, a company has a manageable number of products or services that solve problems. They commercialize those products or services to maximize the return on investment. Then, approximately two years before the end of a product's lifecycle, they start to develop its replacement.

Barrood: What about the people part of the innovation process? How important is it to trust your team, and to have a team with diverse backgrounds that bring different skills to the table?

> **Bailye:** That's a great question. One other element of successful, innovative leadership is the ability to delegate. As Dendrite grew, I gave decision-making authority in the areas of innovation to smaller teams. I took those teams out of the traditional reporting structure and had them report to me on a weekly basis. They took more ownership of managing a specific product. I've used many different methods managing innovation. None have been as productive as giving a small team more ownership of a product or program with direct reporting responsibility to the top. They believed they played an integral role in the success of the product—and they did.

Barrood: Lastly, what advice would you give to current business leaders and entrepreneurs about innovation and being innovative leaders?

> **Bailye:** Today's innovative leaders must stay in touch with their customers. They must be confident in their ability to successfully lead a growing company. And they must know when to empower members of the team so that innovative thinking drives new solutions for existing problems.

CHAPTER 2

The Path to Entrepreneurship:
Seven Rules for Business Success

By Maxine Ballen, president and CEO,
New Jersey Technology Council

Maxine Ballen

Maxine Ballen gave the Rothman Institute's Fifth Annual Richard M. Clarke Distinguished Entrepreneurial Lecture on May 5, 2003. At the time Ballen was the founder, president and CEO of the New Jersey Technology Council (NJTC), a private, nonprofit member organization composed of technology-intensive and associated companies. Founded in 1996, the Technology Council represents approximately 1,160 members who constitute the dominant technology sectors in the state.

NJTC is Ballen's third nonprofit start-up in support of entrepreneurship. She received the Entrepreneur of the Year Award in Pennsylvania in 1991 and in New Jersey in 1996. In 2002, the Women's Fund of New Jersey presented her with its "Women Advancing Technology" award. Also in 2002, *NJBIZ* designated her as a "Superstar" and among its "Women of Influence."

As of spring 2010, Ballen remains the president and CEO of the New Jersey Technology Council, one of the leading technology associations nationwide.

I can't remember a time when making money didn't matter to me. As a young child, I was always looking for ways to expand my allowance. I couldn't wait to get my first "real job." When my parents gave the go-ahead, I started to babysit and do odd jobs. At 16, I got my first job doing what I've always enjoyed most — selling! Throughout high school, I worked in several retail stores, selling everything from candy to shoes. I loved the independent feeling of having money in my pocket.

Even then, I was drawn to understanding what it took to be an entrepreneur. I found out it's about more than just having a great idea. You have to be willing to take risks and manage the challenges that you face on the path to realizing your dream. You have to be a self-starter who is extremely motivated and really *wants* to succeed.

I think most entrepreneurs come across that one opportunity that speaks to them and says, "This is your time. Go after it. Take a chance. Assume the risks. Be a success." That time came to me in the early 1980's when, Willard Rouse, a great entrepreneur from the famous Rouse real estate family, invited me to come out to suburban Philadelphia and work with him. We created the Business Development and Training Center, one of the first tenant amenities in the country specifically for technology companies.

I know that many of you can't imagine a time when technology did not rule our lives. But back then, no one was that comfortable even saying the word "technology," much less using a computer on a daily basis. What did I know about technology and working with technology companies?

I quickly learned that the needs of tech companies were very different than more traditional companies that most of us knew back then. At the BDTC, we developed special programs, networking opportunities, access to capital — both financial and human — and a newspaper to serve and connect the community.

Working with Rouse was like a light bulb was always on in my head. I couldn't help but get passionate and excited about becoming an entrepreneur myself. I learned that being a true entrepreneur isn't something you can define with just words. According to Webster's dictionary, an entrepreneur is someone who organizes, operates and assumes the risk for a business venture. But, I found out that it's also a fire in the belly and a light in the eyes.

I took to working with technology companies and the techies who ran them like a moth gravitating to a flame. This was where I *needed* to be. I met so many entrepreneurs who positively glowed when they spoke about their products or services. The ones who didn't weren't around long enough to even make a difference. To this day, if I don't see that glow when I meet an entrepreneur, I know he or she shouldn't quit their day job.

While heading up the center in 1985, I started one of the first support groups for entrepreneurs in the country: PIN, the Pennsylvania Innovation Network. Building on PIN's success, I began a similar organization in New Jersey called SJEN — the South Jersey Entrepreneur's Network. I was on my way.

In my life, my mentors helped by example and support. If Bill Rouse helped put me on the ladder, then Edison Venture Fund's John Martinson offered me the opportunity to get to the next rung. John and I met in the '80s when I first started doing venture fairs in New Jersey. As the region's leading venture capitalist, I called on John and asked for his participation and support.

John Martinson is one of the brightest and most enjoyable people I've ever had the opportunity to work with. He urged me to move to

New Jersey to start a statewide entrepreneurial support organization. For a year I said "NO." I was happy at BDTC. But, I caught the entrepreneur's bug – yet again. I turned the Pennsylvania operations over to my staff and started at the beginning once again. The following year, John and I started the New Jersey Technology Council.

What a risk! I was happy and secure living and working in Pennsylvania. Leaving it all and coming to New Jersey to start a new venture wasn't easy. But, when people ask me if I would do it again, there's no question in my mind; the answer is *"Yes!"* Watching the Council grow from a great idea to a $2.5 million organization with almost 1,200 members has been one of the most gratifying experiences of my life.

If I make it sound as though the recipe for entrepreneurial success is simple, then forgive me. It's actually so complex and daunting, that few people do more than dream about it, and even fewer are successful. If you decide to make the journey, there are some things you need in your "briefcase" before you even try to take your show on the road.

First, you need to be flexible. No successful innovator made it without the ability to take risks and accept change. The passion to make things happen despite the odds is essential, and so is the ability to communicate your passion to others.

Once you do make it, you need to keep the fires burning — the fire in your own soul and the flame that attracts people to your doorstep. The best way to do that is to have your own personal rules for business success. Here are my seven rules:

» Focus on your own definition of success. Would you rather have a small piece of a big pie or 100 percent of nothing?

» Never lose your enthusiasm for what you are doing. The minute it is no longer fun for you, get out. You better be the primary cheerleader for your staff, your members or customers and everyone else with whom you come in contact. The minute you lose that, you should get going yourself.

» Build high-quality teams with complementary skills. We've all heard that a chain is only as strong as its weakest link. Hire the best and the brightest you can afford because the quality of your staff determines your success. Make sure you provide the best benefits and quality of work life you can afford. Your employees will stay with you and work even harder. Some of the most successful companies in the country are great examples of this principle and include: SAS, Merck and Knight-Ridder.

» Once you have the best people on your team, treat them well. Treat people the way you want to be treated yourself. Never lose sight of that. I don't care what position the person may occupy, from custodian on up. They are just as important as you. If they don't do their job, you can't do your job.

» Reward and celebrate success. The best managers give credit where credit is due and share the blame when things go wrong.

» Never neglect the basic housekeeping rules of business. Return all phone calls. Respond to e-mails in a timely manner. Don't ignore traditional forms of communications. There is no excuse these days for being unreachable – especially to your staff. Unless I'm on vacation, which I rarely am, I return all phone calls and e-mails by sunset – every day. People deserve to receive a response even if they are trying to sell you something. We are all selling something at one time or another. The only thing worse than being ignored is ignoring someone.

» Value your family and your personal life. I have been very fortunate in having a support system in place that has allowed me to get to this point in my life.

In retrospect, it's funny to think that the woman with the "show me the money" mantra likes the world of non-profit. Can you imagine? *Not* making a profit? Of course, as we know, there's tremendous profit to be made in the non-profit world. And it's not always green.

These days, at the New Jersey Technology Council, I absolutely love seeing the look on an entrepreneur's face when I can help them access a new path to potential financing, or introduce them to their next customer. I have founded several entrepreneurial ventures, and there is nothing more satisfying than seeing them live on and survive well *after* you've stepped aside.

CHAPTER 3

Plan to Succeed

By Reginald Best, president and COO of ProtonMedia,
and founder and former CEO of Netilla Networks

Reginald Best

Reginald Best gave the Rothman Institute's Sixth Annual Richard M. Clarke Distinguished Entrepreneurial Lecture on May 3, 2004. At that time Best was the co-founder, president and CEO of Netilla Networks Inc., a technology start-up that has become one of the leading global providers of remote access systems. Founded in 1999, Netilla develops and markets networking products that allow a company's employees to securely log into their business networks from anywhere using just a web browser.

Netilla is the third tech start-up for Best, a recognized entrepreneur in the networking industry. After beginning his career at AT&T Bell Laboratories, Best formed his first venture, Teleos Communications, a video-networking company that was sold to Madge Networks. He then founded AccessWorks Communications, an Internet/remote access company acquired by 3Com Corporation. Best was named one of "40 Under 40" by *NJBIZ* magazine, highlighting him as one of the state's top young business leaders.

As of spring 2010, Best is the president and COO of ProtonMedia. He left AEP Systems in 2009, the company he stayed on with after it had acquired Netilla in 2006. He oversees day-to-day operations, marketing and venture capital initiatives as well as the launch of ProtoSphere 2.0, the company's state-of-the-art social environment for online teaming.

One of the things that I have learned about tech start-ups over the years is that this stuff is hard. There aren't a lot of people who do it, and there's a good reason for that. Every day you are close to the brink of disaster. There is always a problem, an issue or something that has to be tackled. But entrepreneurs thrive on chaos. We have to be focused on the business while carefully watching our expenses. Everyday, someone in my company is telling me, *"If we invest here, then this is how much more we could get in six months."* I usually reply, *"If we did that, in six months we might not be in business."*

I'm a firm believer that cash is king. To be successful, you must manage it effectively. As we all know, business partnerships are important for early stage companies; the financial strength of your partners is a critical component of the partnership. I am proud to say that, in four years of active retailing at Netilla, we've had one bad debt, and even that one was painful for us to swallow.

Part of our success has come from focusing on key sweet spots. Our business expanded, sometimes over the objections of our investors, into international markets more quickly than we expected. We were selling in the U.S. and growth was OK, but the real opportunity was overseas. I came from a company that did 50% of its business outside the United States. Additionally, we needed to establish a presence in Europe and Asia; otherwise we risked being locked out of those markets. If we wanted the additional revenue opportunities in our market, we had to go and get them; they weren't coming to us.

Another part of our success came from our willingness to change over time. If you looked at my business plan in 1999, it was completely different than what we wound up actually doing. As one of my investors said, "We made it by our ability to zig as well as zag through the process." That's what investors look for when putting their money into companies—people's ability to recognize changes and shifts, and to successfully move with them in the marketplace.

At Netilla, we typically adjust our plans on a quarterly basis, depending on what is happening in the market and at our monthly board meetings. As a business, we established a mission and a general course. But, there is a lot of fine tuning that goes on underneath the surface, and that often happens on a weekly basis.

The only real advantage that a small company has is its ability to move quickly and react to market trends and changes. Big companies have more money and more people, but if you have a small business you can come back from a customer meeting and change plans on a dime; you can win the business if you execute properly after you make that decision. Big companies are like those big oil tankers; you have to stop them five miles out so they can coast in to port.

I think entrepreneurship will continue to be a critical component of the U.S. economy. Opportunities abound, but there is global competition and global demand. We must recognize this aspect of our business and plan accordingly. Given how the pendulum has swung, I believe it's time for back-to-business basics. Find good customers that make you happy and pay their bills on time.

There is always opportunity for the next generation of business leaders in networking communications and computer communications companies. We are just scratching the surface. We are the Ford Model T in our industry. There are many undiscovered, innovative ideas out there. In the interim, below are three rules that I have learned over the years, especially in my time with Netilla:

Don't take too long to get out to the marketplace and try stuff out. It's important to know quickly whether or not the dogs are going to eat the dog food; whether you are going to actually be able to get some sales traction and sell something.

Quickly find your customers. You can't do it alone inside the company, and increasingly you can't do it alone outside the company. You need both internal and external partners to help build the business. Most entrepreneurs need help in this area if they are going to survive.

Find honest critics. In the early stages of a business, it's important to find an adviser, a group and/or someone who has already done what you want to do. Show them your plan and let them poke holes in it to make your idea better. At some point, you will need to communicate your idea to the investor community and to your customers. Can you successfully defend your mission statement? Can you explain your business in ways that people outside your business will understand it? If not, how can you expect someone to invest in your company or buy your product?

One important rule that falls outside the business plan, that is just as critical as anything in it is: don't forget about your family while you're trying to live the American dream. In the end, you are only truly successful if you've properly managed the business/personal parts of your life. If the people closest to you aren't part of the dream, then all the business success you achieve will mean nothing. You will have sacrificed too much.

CHAPTER 4

The Thrills and Chills of Building a High-Tech Company

By Ken Burkhardt, president of Verbier Ventures,
and co-founder of Dialogic Corporation

Ken Burkhardt

Dr. Kenneth J. Burkhardt Jr. gave the Rothman Institute's Second Annual Richard M. Clarke Distinguished Entrepreneurial Lecture on March 30, 2000. At the time Burkhardt had just left Intel, which had acquired Dialogic Corporation in 1999. He co-founded Dialogic, and from 1983 to 1992 was executive vice president of operations. From 1992 to the acquisition of Dialogic by Intel in July 1999, he was executive vice president of New Business Development.

From July until February 2000, he was a member of Intel Capital, Intel Corporation's investment arm. From 2000 to 2005 he was chairman of the board and CEO of Aloha Networks Inc., a venture-backed company that developed products for the satellite communications industry.

As of spring 2010, Burkhardt is the president of Verbier Ventures, LLC, a consulting and investment management firm, and a director of Octasic, a fabless semiconductor company.

Dialogic Corporation did not evolve perfectly, but I believe that there were a number of things that we did and did not do that led to our success and might serve as a useful guideline for anyone contemplating entering the world of high-tech start-ups, venture capital and the associated highs and lows of a roller coaster ride.

Dialogic was the world market share leader in supplying hardware and software tools for the implementation of automated call-processing systems. Before our acquisition by Intel in July of 1999, we were a NASDAQ-listed company with $300 million in sales. Our primary product line was hardware and software tools for building systems as diverse as low-end automated attendant systems up to central-office-class voice mail and fax mail systems. Our business was connecting any type of data that goes over a telephone line to computers. We do not sell products directly to end users. We provided tools to value-added resellers and original equipment manufacturers ranging in size from AT&T and IBM down to start-up companies.

We evolved through a combination of inspiration, luck, hard work and timing. Thomas Edison once said, "*Success is 10 percent inspiration and 90 percent perspiration.*" In our case, I would modify the adage by saying that success was due to 10 percent inspiration, 30 percent perspiration and 60 percent luck or timing.

Dialogic was formed in June of 1983 by three people: Jim Shinn, a Princeton and Harvard Business School graduate who had an international banking and foreign relations background and was at the time the Advanced Micro Devices area sales manager, Nick Zwick, a Stony Brook MS in electrical engineering who was the local AMD field applications engineering manager, and me. After receiving my Ph.D. from the University of Washington in computer science, I spent seven years teaching computer architecture at Rutgers. At the same time, I was a senior system architect in the workstation group at Unisys.

Initially, the division of labor was for Jim to run marketing and sales, Nick was responsible for production and hardware engineering and I was oversaw finance and operations. I knew very little about either of these areas, but as I discovered, they were key to the success of the company. Failure in these two areas is probably the biggest reason that most start-up companies go out of business. They are also the areas most foreign to tech entrepreneurs. Lots of people have good ideas with great technological vision and execution capabilities. However, without strong financial management and a good operations team to support the growth of the company, many start-ups will die an early death.

The technological inspiration for Dialogic's product line was a clever little chip introduced by OKI Semiconductor in 1982. The chip was an OKI 5218 — a part that had the capability to accept a voice data stream and compress it using a variant of the ADPCM voice-encoding standard. Our market inspiration was that a little bit of glue logic, a single chip microprocessor and this OKI part would allow us to build a tool kit that, together with a simple PC, would enable a large number of small companies, hobbyists and entrepreneurs to grow the whole industry.

Given this idea and a few $500 ads in *Byte* magazine, we thought that we could build a $10 million company in five years, take it public and then move onto the next great inspiration. Needless to say, there were a few changes and challenges along the way.

When we started Dialogic, we thought it would be relatively easy to raise money. We had a good business plan that showed solid growth in an area that was hot, and we all had solid resumes. Our plan was to finance the company ourselves for a year, and then get VC money after generating revenue from sales.

We were in for several big surprises. We had significant interest from both large and small venture firms. Despite a lot of dancing, we could not raise any funds during the early stages of company development. The major obstacle for VC people that actually read our business plan was that none of us had ever before started a high-tech company. It was a Catch-22 situation. If we had started a successful, high-tech company, the $1 million that we were looking to raise would have come from our own pockets.

We learned a valuable lesson from the experience. Although VCs can be helpful with initial funding, recruiting and a variety of other intangible areas of business, not getting external financing also has many benefits. In our case, it made us focus on our market strategy and product plans. We had to institute strong financial controls early on in the company's growth cycle. The decision was relatively easy to implement a lean and mean corporate structure with risks and rewards shared by everyone. And there were plenty of risks. During the first three years of the company, we had board meetings every two weeks. The final question of the meeting was always, "*Well Ken, how much money do we owe this week?*" It was a little scary at times, but with careful budgeting, we never missed a payroll or had to take out second mortgages on our houses. We invested nowhere near $1 million, but still managed to successfully execute our early business plan.

Having ideas and funds is the easiest part of building a company. Finding and retaining people to fulfill a vision is the real challenge. Employees will ultimately determine the success or failure of an entrepreneurial venture. Having a defined personnel policy and a goal for a corporate culture are keys to being successful. We chose a very flat Silicon Valley model. Dialogic would not be a place with reserved parking spots and options and profit sharing only for executives. We expected hard work and long hours from everyone. That said, once we were profitable, all employees would share in the benefits, including: stock options, fully paid health care and other benefits such as short-term profit sharing. Furthermore, a key part of our early corporate charter was that working at Dialogic should be fun.

We based the growth of our company on building a strong nucleus of people that would allow us to progress beyond the start-up phase. Our first key hire was an office manager. She was an ex-Air Force woman who did everything from answering the phone to taking orders; shipping product to collecting money. Unless you are excited about ordering stationary and pencils, finding out where best to rent furniture and assorted other time-consuming operations, you better find someone good, capable and honest to fill this position.

Our next three hires were key people to head up hardware engineering, software engineering and manufacturing. All three of the founders had some experience in each of these areas from a prototype/small-volume standpoint. These three hires brought the necessary expertise to allow us to build high volumes of reliable product.

One of our first 10 employees, and the person who made my life much easier, was our Controller. When he joined the company, I stopped worrying about day-to-day accounting issues. He was a young guy, with a few years of public accounting, who grew to become CFO of a public company.

The final founding member of management was our Director of Human Resources. I remember reading that, once a company has 25 people, it needs to have a dedicated person to hiring, retaining and educating the workforce. Our director of HR was employee No. 25 and she was desperately needed. She was another person who had never done the job before, but had the personality to thrive when given a challenge, and to be a true employee advocate to senior management. With this team in place, we were ready to conquer the world.

During the first eight years of our existence, Dialogic was run as a triumvirate. There was no outside board, and decisions were made on a consensus basis with input from employees. Final decisions were made by the three of us. Initially, this worked quite well. But, as sales exceeded $20 million, it became clear that this was a difficult way to do business. We spent too much time developing formal plans, designing a formal mission statement and putting formal, senior manager career-planning in place. Without having one person who had the responsibility and authority of making final decisions, we were often in a mode of *paralysis by analysis*. It was obvious that, to continue the company's growth over $100 million, we needed someone with authority and responsibility for the whole operation.

The real decision point toward radically changing our mode of operations was in March of 1991. Dialogic was invited to give a company presentation at Hambrecht and Quist's annual technology conference at the St. Francis Hotel in San Francisco. By this time, there was a lot of interest in our company. After the presentation, we were sipping a good bottle of wine in the lobby of the St. Francis when Jim raised the key question. *"Well, I guess we're a real company now. Who wants to run this thing?"* The response from all three of us was, *"Not me."* It wasn't that we didn't enjoy the company or the challenges. It was a combination of two things. First, 80-hour weeks are fine for a while, but after five-plus years they start to get old. Second, none of us had run a $100 million company before. We all believed that someone with experience was needed to take Dialogic to the next level. The unanimous decision was to bring someone in from the outside to grow the company.

Mechanically, this was a straightforward, but certainly not trivial issue. There were two recruiting tasks required. First, find and recruit a seasoned CEO who had similar visions as the founders. Second, find and recruit senior executives to help serve on a Board of Directors to sanity-check plans and monitor execution of those plans. Intellectually, this was probably the hardest thing that we did at the company. We were bringing in someone to take over our jobs. He would have the authority to run our baby on a day-to-day basis. Furthermore, by putting in place an independent board, we were instituting a formal process of monitoring his performance and running the company at a top level where we would only have a vote, but not absolute authority. This was the point where we all made the decision to sweep our egos out the door — easier said than done, but crucial to lifting the company to its present state.

We found an excellent CEO within three-months. Initially he was put in charge of research and development. After a year, he was given operations, followed by the rest of the company in late 1993. Each of the founders took different roles as the process evolved. Nick became Chairman of the Board and concentrated his non-board related efforts on corporate legal and patent issues. I went from being VP of Operations to VP of Business Development. Jim stayed on the board, but left the company to work at the Council on Foreign Relations.

For anyone starting a business today, I would offer them the following six guidelines that helped us successfully build our company:

1. Write and annually rewrite business plans. Continual updating of a complete strategic plan is critical to success. If nothing else, finding holes in your plan will pinpoint areas where you need help.

2. Define your corporate culture up front and make sure that you believe in it.

3. Carefully evaluate funding alternatives in terms of your business plan.

4. Make sure that you understand your value added.

5. Hire great people.

6. Be prepared to continue your education.

Building a company in a fast-changing market was an exciting and rewarding experience. Advanced academic study gave me excellent training because it offered experience in discovering and researching subjects about which I knew very little. *If you are willing to recognize what you don't know, the road to success becomes much clearer.*

CHAPTER 5

The Evolution of an Innovative Business Unit

By Charles Cascio, vice president of
partnership expansion at Educational Testing Service

Charles Cascio

Charles Cascio spoke at the Rothman Institute's Third Annual Innovation Conference on September 23, 2008. At the time Cascio was vice president of interactive learning, going beyond the traditional assessments to help deliver learning through the Internet, hand-held devices, and other multimedia technologies.

He joined ETS in 2000 as director of special projects, coordinating a corporate image campaign and increasing visibility for ETS' education reform activities. He led many initiatives, creating the first companywide sales force, heading the Communications & Public Affairs Division, and incubating and creating the Interactive Learning Division in 2007.

Before joining ETS, Cascio was vice president for certification standards and teacher development at the National Board for Professional Teaching Standards (NBPTS). He created standards-based products and services, established the NBPTS National Institutes program, and directed other higher education initiatives.

As of spring 2010, Cascio is vice president of partnership expansion, where he leads ETS into markets outside of the traditional education sectors.

For 60 years ETS has advanced quality and equity in education through fair and valid assessments, research and related services. It administers 50 million assessments yearly in more than 180 countries and has won awards for innovative use of new technologies for computer and Internet-based testing.

Educational Testing Service is a not-for-profit organization. We are the world leader in educational testing and research, and we administer more than 50 million tests annually worldwide. Since 2000, we have seen our revenues grow from $400 million to $1.3 billion. We like to think of ourselves as a 61-year-old *new* company. Our mission is to take our resources and put them in position to provide cutting-edge solutions to learning in different environments, in different capacities and through different technologies.

In 2000, ETS reached a historical turning point. Before then, ETS had always been led by persons with academic backgrounds. If you have ever been to our headquarters in Princeton, New Jersey, it looks very much like a university setting. In July, 2000, however, the board of trustees hired Kurt Landgraf as president and CEO. He was not an educator — though he did lead education reform when he was an executive at DuPont Europe. Kurt had the business acumen and penchant for innovation necessary to kick ETS up to the next level of operation, while maintaining a strong commitment to its educational mission.

Most of you have been vetted, in one way or another, by ETS at some point in your careers. You took the PSAT, or the SAT, or the GRE, all core businesses for ETS. When Kurt came aboard, he decided to preserve the core brands, but also wanted to put together a plan for growth. He set about to change the culture inside ETS. Instead of dictating to markets what they should be doing, ETS listened to the markets and used that information to decide where *we* should be going.

ETS is now consolidated into two large strategic business units: higher education and school assessments, and business development, partnerships and global division. My start-up operation, which is only 18 months old, falls into the second group, the business development and partnerships.

During the current eight-year period of innovation and creative thinking, our researchers uncovered some disturbing numbers: 70% of high school graduates lack fundamental applied skills. And in fact only 70% of the kids who enter high school in the United States graduate (the numbers for minority populations are much lower). Looking at these statistics, how, as a leading, educational organization, are we addressing the fact that 40% of employers say graduates lack basic reading, writing and math skills? And 81% of employers say that graduates lack basic English writing skills? Employers say that students also lack knowledge of foreign languages and cultures, and awareness of the global market.

Employers of hourly workers tell us that they are rejecting applicants because of inadequate basic employability skills. When we heard that, we discovered even more disturbing statistics. In 1979, 49% of all teens were employed in some capacity. By the year 2000, it had dropped to 45%, but in 2004 it was 36%, and preliminary statistics from 2007 show it's down to just above 30%. The largest decline of employability in any age group is among teenagers.

If teenagers are not in school, and they are not able to find jobs, what does that mean to their communities? We examined the situation and created a research report called "America's Perfect Storm: *Three Forces Changing Our Nation's Future.*" The report analyzes the convergence of education, demographic and economic forces and the fact that these forces are causing a critical decline in U.S. global competitiveness. (The report can be downloaded from the ETS website, www. ets.org.)

In 2006, I was in charge of incubating the Family Market Initiative. In my role, I talked to businesses about whether ETS could actually play in the commercial market space outside of education. Could we work with companies interested to see how ETS' intellectual property might be embedded into things like mobile devices, game technology, interactive computers and so forth? We signed two major contracts during the first year. The deals motivated us to establish the Interactive Learning Strategic Business Unit in January 2007. We looked at game technology, and we looked at mobile technology. Soon, we will sign an agreement with a major mobile device carrier in China, where people will be able to access English-language learning from their cell phones and practice it as they are walking around.

The small team that I head at ETS has come up with many ideas in 18 months. We have talked with 70 potential partners, ranging from a small game-making company operating out of a garage in Santa Monica, to Microsoft and Apple. Here are some of the things that are emerging out of Interactive Learning:

> WHAMI stands for "Who am I?" It is a series of non-cognitive assessments that kids can take but that feels like they are playing a game. In our pilot program, I was stunned that kids would sit calmly for over an hour answering questions about themselves. At the end of the interview, they got a profile of their learning strengths. Parents can use the profile to analyze such things as how to set up a child's room so the learning environment is more conducive to her likes and dislikes.

» Proofwriter is an online writing tool that provides students with quick feedback on grammar usage, mechanics and style. If you've ever had trouble with a report or a memo that you were writing and wanted a quick critique, Proofwriter would do that for you in a matter of seconds.

» Jabara is a mystery game where kids can pick a super hero to take them through a number of spelling and grammar lessons by interacting with them in a mobile device that talks back to them. It will say, "No, you need to try that again," and it keeps track of the player's score.

There is a perfect storm in education right now and it's not pretty. We have what Tom Friedman calls a "flat world" flooded with opportunity. But there is a radical evolution going on that will engage industries by changing the corporate environment into a learning institution. When we look at all that ETS can bring through innovation, we are looking at a world of potential for interactive learning, for research and development, and for everybody who engages in learning and education.

CHAPTER 6

Disruptive Innovation

By Clayton Christensen, renowned author, consultant and
Harvard Business School professor and
Michael Horn, co-founder and executive director of
Education of Innosight Institute and author

Clayton Christensen

Clayton Christensen presented at the Rothman Institute's Innovation Summit on April 6, 2006. At the time he was Robert and Jane Cizik Professor of Business Administration at the Harvard Business School. He is one of the most sought-after business consultants in the innovation area and is an adviser to some of America's most successful companies. His research and teaching interests center on the management issues related to the development and commercialization of technological and business model innovation. Christensen is the author of the bestselling books: *The Innovator's Dilemma* (1997), which received the Global Business Book Award for the best business book published in 1997, and *The Innovator's Solution* (2003), which appeared in the *BusinessWeek* bestseller list. More recent books have included *Seeing What's Next*, published in 2004, *Innovator's Prescription - A Disruptive Solution for Health Care*, published in 2008, and *Disrupting Class: How Disruptive Innovation Will Change the Way the World Learns*, published in 2009.

Michael B. Horn

Michael B. Horn presented at the Rothman Institute's Innovation Summit on April 14, 2010. At the time, he led the Innosight Institute, a not-for-profit think tank devoted to applying the theories of disruptive innovation to problems in the social sector. He is the coauthor of *Disrupting Class: How Disruptive Innovation Will Change the Way the World Learns* with Harvard Business School Professor and bestselling author Clayton Christensen and Curtis W. Johnson. *BusinessWeek* named the book one of the 10 Best Innovation & Design Books of 2008, *Strategy + Business* awarded it the best human capital book of 2008, and *Newsweek* named it as the 14th book on its list of "Fifty Books for Our Times." The book uses the theories of disruptive innovation to identify the root causes of schools' struggles and suggests a path forward to customize an education for every child in the way he or she learns. Horn has been a featured keynote speaker at many conferences including the Virtual School Symposium and Microsoft's School of the Future World Summit. He has also has written articles for numerous publications, including *Education Week*, *Forbes*, the *Boston Globe*, and *U.S. News & World Report*.

When you look back across the sweep of business history, many companies that were once widely regarded as unassailably successful seem to drop precipitously to the middle of the pack or even fall to the bottom of the heap. Why does this happen? What kills successful companies?

After studying the problem for six years, I came to realize that the principles of good management, which are taught at every business school, are usually responsible for sowing the seeds of most companies' ultimate demise. As a result, the term *innovation*, or a company's attempt to create new growth businesses, has acquired a stench of randomness and risk. As we've studied innovation, however, what we've seen is that innovation doesn't have to be so unpredictable if you follow good theory.

When starting a business, one of the first questions most people ask themselves is, *How do we beat the competition?* In order to respond accurately to the question, you need good theory. The theory can help us think our way through many of the questions we have when launching a new, entrepreneurial venture.

The first element of our theory or model is that in every market there is a trajectory of performance improvement that customers can utilize. Every year, car companies give us new and improved engines, but we can't fully access their power because of things like police on the road putting a crimp on how much performance we can use.

The second element of our model is that in each market there is a trajectory of improvement that companies provide as they keep introducing new, improved products. The most important part of the second element is that the trajectory of technological improvement almost always outstrips the ability of customers to use the improvement.

In the 1980s, when we first used word processing programs, the Intel 286 chip wasn't fast enough for typing. Today, Intel's 3 GH, Pentium 4 processor has overshot the speed that most customers can use.

Some innovations that help companies move up the trajectory are just simple engineering advances; others are dramatic breakthrough technologies. However, they both have the same effect on the market structure in sustaining the trajectory of performance improvement as it existed in the market at the time.

Invariably, the firms that are leaders before the battles of sustaining innovation began find themselves still on top when those battles are over. Technologically speaking, the complexities of the new innovations were irrelevant. In our study, if the purpose of the innovation was to create an improved product that could sell for more attractive profits to their best customers, the company would figure out a way to do it.

We also observed that, on occasion, new and different kinds of technology came into industries. We call these types of innovations a *disruptive technology*. We coined the term not because the technology is a breakthrough improvement, but rather it brings a product to the market that is not as good, but it is simple, affordable and can take root in an undemanding application and then improve. Most entrant companies that go to market with disruptive innovations usually end up killing the incumbent leaders. That is the basic model.

In an early meeting with Intel Chairman Andy Grove, we discussed disruptive technology. With a puzzled look on his face, he said, *"I see where your theory is wrong."* He pointed to the words disruptive technologies and said *"Clay, if I have you right, if you call it disruptive technology, you are going to mislead people."*

Unfortunately, I had used the term in my recently published book, *The Innovator's Dilemma*. Andy continued, *"I think it would be more accurate to characterize it as 'trivial technology' that disrupts the business model of the leader and that is what makes it so hard."* He went on to give his view of the puzzle that served as our original motivation for the study. We talked about Digital Equipment Corp., a huge minicomputer company that collapsed in the late 1980s.

In the 1970s and 80s, Digital Equipment Corp. was one of the most widely admired companies in the world. It went from start-up to $15 billion in revenue and became a powerful force in the world of technology. The main driver for Digital's success was said to be its top-notch management team.

In 1988, Digital fell off a cliff. The main reason given by analysts and industry experts was the "ineptitude" of the management team— the very same people lauded for their performance earlier in the decade.

How did such good managers get so stupid so fast? Or, is it possible that there were other factors in the death of Digital Equipment Corp.? We questioned the "bad management" hypothesis. At the time, every minicomputer company was collapsing in unison. It wasn't just Digital, but also companies like Data General, Hewlett-Packard and Wang. You might expect these companies to collude on pricing occasionally, but to collude on collapsing was a stretch. There was something more fundamental going on in the tech industry.

Andy looked at Digital's history through the lens of our model on why the tech companies collapsed together. He said, *"If you line up the sequence of computers that Digital introduced to its markets in 1970s and 1980s, and then unscrew the cover to look at the technologies that were acquired to make a good minicomputer better, they didn't skip a beat. Digital did everything they could to make better products that they could sell for higher margins to their best customers."*

Andy reminded me about the sub-standard quality of the first personal computers. One example was Apple, which sold the Apple II computer as a toy to children. None of Digital's customers could use a personal computer in the first decade of their existence. No one foresaw that a personal computer could take root as a toy, and then improve to the point where it would meet mainstream needs later.

Andy concluded that, *"It wasn't technology that was the problem. Digital's engineers were dealing with much more complicated technologies than were required to make a PC. In fact, they could design a PC with their eyes shut, but they had a business model [which dictated how they made money], and [that model] simply couldn't prioritize this"* because selling a PC was not profitable in their model.

Digital did everything that Wall Street wanted them to do. They focused on their best customers, got out of low-margin profits and invested in technology with higher margins. They also vacated the bottom of the technology market. There was an asymmetry of motivation, which occurs when a company is motivated to move into a market and their competitor is motivated to move out of it.

Disruption in Education

We see many instances of disruptive innovation happening right now in education—in the K-12 sector, higher education, and professional development. And if we want to see transformation in our education system, disruption can be a catalyst to accelerate that process.

Reform efforts in education have been around for decades. There's a great book called *Tinkering Toward Utopia* that discusses all the various newfangled reform efforts throughout history. And yet despite these efforts, we haven't seen fundamental transformation. Our system was built as a factory model system—to treat every student within cohorts in the same way. We teach the same subjects, in the same way, on the same day. We have pacing guides and standardized tests at the end of each class.

This monolithic system would be fine if all students learned in the exact same way or had the same passions, interests and motivations. But, as we all know from our own experiences, that just isn't the case. As a result, we should have a system that offers custom solutions for those differences. Unfortunately, the solutions would be prohibitively expensive to enact in the current system.

By migrating student education to the computer—to online learning—teachers can offer customized pathways that allow students to explore subjects in depth. Additionally, they can create things and collaborate with people not just in their classroom, which may become an outdated concept, but across the world.

Computers have been around for several decades, but they haven't had a transformational impact in our education system. Today, computers are used as a layer on top of the education system to sustain what we already do, but they don't fundamentally transform the process of learning. Our leaders in education are cramming them into the existing model rather than disruptively deploying them. In a new education model, computers would compete against areas of nonconsumption at the outset, just as Apple started by selling its computers as toys to children, who couldn't afford Digital Equipment Corp.'s minicomputers.

In the U.S., pockets of nonconsumption can be found in all areas at the course level. Online learning would effectively penetrate these areas. One example is home-schooled and home-bound students. Much of the disruptive innovation in education started with virtual schools in the form of virtual charter schools. Companies like K12 Inc.

and Connections Academy have been pioneers in this area.

Another area is in advanced courses as well as scheduling conflicts. State virtual schools that offered supplemental courses served these areas from the outset. Florida and Michigan have made great strides in the area of nonconsumption in education. The Florida Virtual School offers classes to students that might have been cut from a brick-and-mortar school's curriculum. Today, there are 34 AP courses. Florida schools can't offer all 34 AP courses to their students. But, there are always kids interested in AP classes that are not offered. Rather than hire a full-time instructor, schools turn to a virtual teacher reaching many students in different towns and cities around the state.

Nationally, 25 percent of American high schools don't offer an advanced course defined as anything above geometry or biology—so no chemistry, no physics—and no honors English classes. This disproportionately affects small rural and urban schools.

As the offerings for online learning become more robust, they offer multiple pathways for students to learn in the ways that make sense for them. The biggest areas of growth for online learning now are in credit recovery and among dropouts.

Credit recovery is any instance when a student fails a course and has no recourse to make it up. In most urban districts, when this happens the student just moves on. This is a big problem because failing students don't get the learning they need for future opportunities. They also don't get the credits needed to graduate. It feeds the dropout problem, which is another big area of nonconsumption.

Unit recovery is an interesting area of nonconsumption that we didn't think about when we wrote *Disrupting Class*. If a student fails a particular project or module, rather than move them onto the next one as our system does today, we should give them the opportunity to make it up online and get the learning they need from the class.

Disaster preparedness has become a big area of discussion, particularly with the current administration. When schools shut down, either because of man-made or natural disasters, learning for many children shuts down as well. Online education provides continuity when teaching in the classroom isn't an option. The concept is starting to gain traction in schools that deal with disaster planning on an annual basis.

Whenever we see disruptive innovation, it follows an S-curve pattern. In high schools, we are forecasting that 50 percent of all courses will be delivered online by 2019. That's nine or 10 years from now, which means for education that would be a relatively fast change.

We see the same disruptive phenomenon happening in higher education. In the 1600s, higher education started by serving a small, affluent population at places such as Harvard University. Most people didn't have access to higher education; it was very centralized. The Land Grant Acts of the 1800s opened up education for a whole new swath of society in the birth of state universities. Following in their footsteps were community colleges.

Today, over 50 percent of post-secondary education in the U.S. takes place at community colleges. It is decentralizing relative to state universities. The next big wave, online universities, is competing on a convenience or access dimension. The new, online educational programs allow more people to access higher education for the first time or for job retraining, and they can do it in the comfort of their own homes or workplaces.

Online universities are growing rapidly. Between 2007 and 2009, a period when the economy was contracting and people were expected to rush back to school, higher education enrollments grew by a paltry

1.2 percent. Online education enrollments, however, increased 17 percent. Most experts peg annual industry growth now at 19 to 20 percent.

Today, 9 percent of physicians receive their continuing medical education online. A new study by John Harris projects that by 2016, using the methodology of the S-curve, about 50 percent of continuing medical education will be online. It's radically changing the field with interesting implications for hospitals. They can now offer training for a lot less money and more conveniently for health-care professionals needing continuing medical education credentials.

We're also seeing online education growing in the area of professional development. In 2006, 40 percent of all professional development for corporations occurred online.

Can Established Organizations Disrupt Themselves, or Are They Always Disrupted?

It turns out that there have been a few companies that have survived attacks of disruption; some have even thrived. But, in every case, they survived by setting up a totally autonomous business unit under a corporate umbrella and giving it an unfettered charter to kill the parent.

In the 1960s, department stores such as Macy's had a full line of hard goods and soft goods. They sold everything from paint to hardware, sporting goods to kitchen utensils, and clothes to toys. Wal-Mart, Target and Kmart came in as discount retailers and challenged the hard-goods end of Macy's business. Back in the 1960s, Target and Wal-Mart had almost no clothing. As their hard-goods business grew, the department stores were relieved to move upmarket and focus on soft goods. They understood that the margin on hard goods was 20 percent compared to 40 to 60 percent margins in soft goods such as clothing and cosmetics.

The people who go into Macy's today and see it as a clothing and cosmetics store don't realize how much the store was disrupted. Of the 316 department stores that populated the industry in 1960, only one made the transition to discount retailing. Dayton-Hudson in Minneapolis made the jump when they set up a separate division called Target.

As soon as discount retailers drove the department stores out of the hard goods market, prices collapsed. The market got worse when retailers such as Home Depot, Circuit City and Staples joined the fray. Their entry forced companies like Target to move into the world of clothing and use their tremendous cost advantage to compete against Macy's.

Today, online retailing is emerging as the disruptive force relative to the discount retail stores. Just witness the explosive growth of Amazon.com and other online retailers. Where did they tend to start? With the lower-margin hard goods. And today they have moved relentlessly upmarket such that you can buy many higher-margin items online, too—including clothing and cosmetics.

So as you can see, disruptive innovation is constantly at work in every part of our economy and society—from technology-heavy industries to education to the world of retail. It is the engine—or causal mechanism—behind the term that the great economist Joseph Schumpeter coined several decades ago, *creative destruction*, and it offers us a way to deliver products and services for lower cost, at higher convenience, and with much greater simplicity and ease. For managers, understanding this theory and these causal forces at play in every realm are vital for making good decisions in leading their companies.

Knowing when disruption is afoot and managing it as an opportunity is not easy, but doing it right is tremendously rewarding for the new growth opportunities it creates.

CHAPTER 7

Mission Driven Innovation

By Douglas Conant, president and
CEO of Campbell Soup Company

Douglas Conant

Douglas Conant gave the Rothman Institute's Second Annual CEO Innovation Lecture on October 25, 2007. At the time Conant was president and chief executive officer of Campbell Soup Company and a director of the company. Conant is Campbell's 11th leader in the company's nearly 140-year history.

Under Conant's leadership, Campbell reversed a precipitous decline in market value and employee engagement. The company made significant investments to improve product quality and packaging, strengthen the effectiveness of its marketing programs, and develop a robust innovation pipeline. Campbell also improved its financial profile, enhanced its relationships with its customers, and consistently improved its employee engagement through investments in its organization.

As of spring 2010, Conant remains president and CEO of one of the world's most successful food companies. He is Chairman and Trustee of The Conference Board and serves on the board of directors of the Committee Encouraging Corporate Philanthropy, the Grocery Manufacturers Association and Students in Free Enterprise.

As a global manufacturer and marketer of simple meals, the Campbell Soup Company generates approximately $8 billion in sales today. With popular brands such as "Pepperidge Farm," "V8", and "Campbell's" soups, our products are sold in more than 120 countries around the world. We employ more than 23,000 employees and have been in business for over 140 years.

From 1990-96, we were one of the best performing food companies in the world. However, we built our company on the back of an aggressive acquisition and pricing strategy that was unsustainable. We lost our ability to grow organically and, when the acquisitions dried up and prices couldn't go any higher, we stumbled. From 1996-2000, Campbell Soup Company was one of the poorest performing food companies in the world, and in desperate need of renewal.

During the period of turmoil at Campbell, I worked at Nabisco. In January, 2001, shortly after Nabisco was acquired by Philip Morris, I became CEO of Campbell. I spent the next six months assessing our situation and came up with a plan to transform our company. The transformation plan had three phases. In the first phase, we needed to go from being uncompetitive everyday to being competitive on a good day. This phase took three years. The second phase had us going from being competitive to being above average everyday and that's what we are today. We're performing well and can finally lift our sights to see the next phase of our company—being the world's most extraordinary food company by nourishing people's lives everywhere every day.

In the first phase, a key objective was to understand how we became so uncompetitive. After a thorough analysis, we found the answers. We had to raise the level of product quality, reenergize the organization and start building our innovation capabilities. Unfortunately, it was not an overnight solution. The situation reminded me of a quote my father often said to me as a teenager, "*Son, you can't talk your way out of something you behaved your way in to; you simply have to behave your way out of it."* The same logic applied to our company. We had four years of poor performance. In a ponderous grocery industry that grows on average 2% a year, change was not happening overnight. We set reasonable and achievable goals. When we brought forward reasonable targets, our company responded because people could envision us becoming competitive on a good day. When we achieved that goal, we raised the bar to be above average and we are now on the path to extraordinary.

Our business model frames how we think about becoming extraordinary. The model is focused on creating extraordinary shareowner value with two pillars underneath it. We focus on winning in the marketplace by outperforming peer companies in our industry. We also focus on winning in the workplace. A company cannot consistently win in the marketplace without having a vibrant, highly-engaged workplace.

We measure our progress against our mission of becoming extraordinary in two ways. We measured against our success model, marketplace and work place. Our primary marketplace measure is total share owner returns. Our goal is to be the best in the decade, not the best in the quarter. But we know that analysts don't want to wait 10 years for us to see how we are doing, so we commit to having our above average rolling three year total share on return every year.

Our primary workplace measure is employee engagement. We look at our engagement relative to other peer companies and the Gallup Q12 Survey, which creates what is known as an engagement ratio. Any population can be broken into three groups, wildly engaged, engaged and actively disengaged. The concept is that you have to have a lot more wildly engaged people than you do actively disengaged. Gallup has measured this over time and found that it directly correlates to creating share owner value, and if you get 12 wildly engaged for every one actively disengaged, then you are world class.

Our goal every year is a continuous improvement goal to do a little better each year than we did the year before. We are winning in the marketplace over the rolling three year period, and in the last three years we are delivering total share on our returns in a challenged industry right now which is 16% per year and that's #1 in our peer group. The most critical measure is our return on invested capital. We had to invest to get the company back on track, but we now have a return on invested capital which is way above where we were originally and growing nicely.

We are also winning in the workplace, and we are maniacal about this. We measure it every year through surveys. Our global leadership team, comprised of the company's top 350 leaders, are now up to a 4.4 out of 5 score in engagement which puts us at the 70th percentile of the executive database. 70% of our top 350 are widely engaged in their work.

Regarding our innovation philosophy, there is a growth imperative in our industry: you either grow or die; there is absolutely nothing in between. There is no compromising innovation; it has to be across your entire value chain, not just in the products you make. It has to be built in to the hearts and minds of the people you work with.

Our innovation is mission driven. The first hurdle that the innovation has to pass is: is it contributing to our ability to build the world's most extraordinary food company? Does it pass the sniff test? If it's not, you have to ask, "Why am I doing it?" Our innovation philosophy is that our challenges to meet the needs of our consumers, customers, employees faster, better and more completely and uniquely than the competition. There is a competitive edge to this innovation game and you want to meet your stake holders' needs, but you have to be viable and it is about speed, quality and completeness.

Our activity across all these areas operates on two levels. One is the innovation level, which is a large scale change impact, where we are doing things that are new to the company or new to the market. But there is also another level of activity that's equally important which is renovation and that's where you are getting incremental changes and incremental impacts that are mission critical, but aren't on a large scale basis.

One of our more recent innovations is microwaveable soups. The first micro-wave was created in 1947. We didn't think seriously about putting soup in a microwaveable container until 55 years later in 2002. We were focused to think we were the world's best can soup company and we were not enlightened on product form. So we launched this product called "Soup at Hand" and then blew it out in terms of variety; now we have a 250 million dollar microwaveable soup business that's growing and attracting a whole new generation of consumers like my children at school.

Another area of innovation is our reduced sodium soups. Sodium is the #1 consumer health concern with soup, especially with senior consumers. The problem is when we take out the sodium, the taste trade off has been too substantial. Fortunately, we've had some break-throughs in sodium reduction, leveraging a special kind of natural sea salt and other technologies, and now offer 43 varieties of low sodium soup which generate over $400 million in sales. It's the fastest growing part of our portfolio.

Our traditional "V8" vegetable juice is recognized for its well-ness credentials, but the flavor and texture is very polarizing with the pretty thick vegetable juice. We saw an opportunity to marry fruits and vegetables and did it with "V8 V Fusion." Consumers now get a full serving of fruit and a full serving of vegetables in every glass. It's a great source of vitamins A, C, and E and has an appealing, sweet flavor with a light texture. People don't know they are drinking vegetables.

Our third area of innovation is our system innovation. Of the 19 largest food companies in the world, 18 of them had an enterprise resource planning system, and ours was the one that didn't. We had 1500 different systems and a rat's nest of management challenges. As a result of this we invested $125 million to establish an enterprise wide planning system. This is as important an innovation as anything we have done on products and the return on this investment will be significant. However, we did have to choose to do it; we did have to make that investment. It would have been easier if I wanted to just be a CEO for three more years to not make this investment and get out, but it was the right thing to do for the business.

The employee engagement process is one of our most relevant areas of innovation. We drive this engagement through a disciplined philosophy where we manage it, measure it and create an action plan around it. The employee engagement process is part of the fabric of our culture, just like any other process, and it helps to drive superior engagement scores. It's another critical element to our mission and our success story.

CHAPTER 8

Extraordinary Measures

by John Crowley, president and CEO of Amicus Therapeutics, Inc.

John Crowley

John Crowley gave the Rothman Institute's Twelfth Annual Richard M. Clarke Distinguished Entrepreneurial Lecture on April 27, 2010. Crowley is an American business and social entrepreneur — and a true inspiration. He is the president and CEO of Amicus Therapeutics, a 100-person publicly held biopharmaceutical company working on the development of drugs to treat a range of human genetic diseases. His involvement in the biotech industry goes back over a decade and stems from the 1998 diagnosis of his two youngest children, Megan and Patrick, with Pompe disease, a rare and fatal neuromuscular disorder.

Crowley embarked on his journey as an entrepreneur to find a treatment that would save his kids' lives — and the lives of thousands of others — parlaying his personal struggles and determination into a series of highly successful biotech business ventures. The movie, *Extraordinary Measures*, was inspired by his true story. Previously, Crowley was founder and CEO at Novazyme Pharmaceuticals and prior to that held several senior positions at Bristol-Myers Squibb.

As of spring 2010, Crowley remains the president and CEO of Amicus Therapeutics.

Extraordinary Measures is a movie based on my family's 12-year journey to find a cure for Pompe disease. In promoting the movie and our cause, I've given hundreds of interviews to media people who all seem to ask the same question, *"What's the movie about?"*

In my replies, I've used many adjectives to elaborate on the film's theme, using family, faith and perseverance, to name a few. In one of my interviews, I said that the movie, more than anything else, is about entrepreneurship.

The comment took me by surprise. I thought about all of the ups and downs since we started our quest. I thought about the successes and failures; two steps forward and one step back. It finally dawned on me that this is how entrepreneurs lead their lives every day.

The title of the movie wasn't confirmed until two months before the marketing started. In focus groups, people came up with titles such as *So Determined* and *So Defiant*. I thought many of the suggestions worked because they accurately described the characteristics of today's entrepreneur. When they finally chose *Extraordinary Measures*, it immediately resonated with me. I saw the title as a testament to the many people who have helped us, over the past 12 years, try to live better lives and be better people.

As I speak here tonight, the press around the movie is just starting to die down. It was introduced in January with the international releases hitting at the end of February. The movie opened in Italy last Friday and I gave a phone interview to a newspaper in Milan. The reporter asked me, "Could your experience have happened in Italy?" I replied, "No, I don't think so. In fact, I don't think it could have happened anywhere else in the world except in America." I explained to the reporter that on our team were private and public companies, academic and government researchers, all working together. We had the federal bureaucracy that approves our drugs help us. We had philanthropists, patient organizations and other families involved as well.

To me, the process was a uniquely American way to solve a complex problem. In tackling a human genetic disease, we not only had to beat nature, we needed to beat time as well.

I once read that entrepreneurs renew society by making products, institutions and practices better. We are the force of creative destruction, while simultaneously creating new ideas, opportunities and business models.

I recently gave a speech at Princeton University to a class of seniors studying entrepreneurship. The professor, Ed Zschau, asked me to talk about my personal experiences in biotech and any life lessons I learned along the way. I shared my perspectives with the class, and spoke about the traits that make a great entrepreneur.

A few days after the event, I received a note from professor Zschau. He wrote that my speech echoed many of the same sentiments that he gives in his annual end-of-the-year speech to students. Entrepreneurship is a state of mind, a state of being. It's constantly looking at problems in life from different vantage points. What entrepreneurship is NOT about ... is money. It's about making a difference in life, and chasing dreams. Capitalism and entrepreneurship aren't about greed. You can be the greediest person in the world, but if you don't know how to compete or how to innovate, you won't make a dime. Conversely, if your focus is not solely based on making money but rather on making great products, providing exceptional service to your customers, and staying ahead of the curve, then before you know it, the wealth will come. What you choose to do with it is up to you.

In reviewing my experiences and discussions over the past decade, I've come to realize that there are four common traits in great entrepreneurs. By understanding these traits and incorporating them into our daily lives, we can achieve a deeper perspective into the true meaning of entrepreneurship.

The first trait of great entrepreneurs is vision. I started my first company, Novazyme Pharmaceuticals, with two partners. We had $37,000 in seed capital and a small lab in Oklahoma. At the time, I lived in Princeton, N.J. Not wanting to uproot my family, I commuted every Monday to Oklahoma City and came home on Friday.

As a company, the first thing we did was sit in a room and talk about where we wanted to be five and 10 years. The answer was easy for me. I wanted to find a cure for Pompe disease, and then come up with technologies to treat a range of human genetic disorders. After that, I was open to suggestions.

As everyone shared their personal goals, we identified similar themes. We used these goals to build the vision for our company. However, we were by no means pioneers in what we were doing.

Let me tell you the story of the very first biotechnology company. In April 1976, Herb Boyer was a researcher working on DNA technologies and recombinant proteins in human genetic engineering to make medicines that extended and enhanced people's lives. He captured the attention of a young venture capitalist at Kleiner Perkins named Bob Swanson. Bob kept pressing Herb because he thought Herb's research would lead to business opportunities. Bob based his vision on research papers he read and academic conferences he attended. Finally, Dr. Boyer agreed to give Bob 10 minutes for his sales pitch. The 10-minute meeting became a three-hour brainstorming session. On the back of a cocktail napkin, they wrote down the vision for what would eventually become the largest biotechnology company in the world. The company was called Genentech.

The second trait of great entrepreneurs is persistence. On my first day at Novazyme, I brought two items with me from New Jersey: a picture of my kids, and a plaque given to me by my mother. The plaque was a quote from Winston Churchill, which read, "Never, never, never quit."

I stared at that plaque many times while in Oklahoma City. Admittedly, I sometimes thought about quitting. I didn't want to be away from my kids. I had trouble raising money. I couldn't pay the company bills or my personal bills. I didn't think I was the smartest or best person for the job. But, looking at that plaque, and repeating those words out loud, made all the difference in the world. When I returned home on Thursday nights, I would see my kids in bed and know what they needed me and our team to do. They needed me to "never, never, never quit." I would persist in the face of failure.

When we agree to become entrepreneurs, we acknowledge the fact that we are going to fail. However, we also agree to learn from our mistakes, move on, and building something great.

One of my other favorite researchers in the biotech world, arguably the first biotech researcher, was Dr. Jonas Salk. Many of you may know him because he invented the vaccine for polio, but he was also someone who never, never, never quit. His original work in the late 1940s at the University of Pittsburgh was funded by a grant from the National Foundation for Infantile Paralysis. He wasn't looking to develop a vaccine. His focus was on doing some epidemiological work, finding out how many people suffered from the different forms of polio.

Dr. Salk had the vision, but he also had persistence in the face of people at his university telling him, "No, you can't go off into research." The people who gave him his grant told him no, as did the people in his own lab.

In the face of repeated failures for developing a vaccine, Dr. Salk continued to persist. For anyone alive back in the early 1950s, polio was a great health scourge of our society. Apart from the atomic bomb, it was probably the greatest fear for people at that time. In 1954, Dr. Salk's drug was approved and polio began to be eradicated from the face of the Earth. As a footnote, he donated the patent to the public domain; he never took any profits from his vaccine. Dr. Salk never, never, never quit.

The third essential trait of great entrepreneurs is optimism. Not only is the glass half full, it's pretty clean too. My wife and I have learned a lot from different people over the past decade. More than anyone else, we've learned from our children. We've learned more about life and love than we've ever taught them.

My daughter has an incredible spirit. Every morning, she comes barreling in her wheelchair to wherever I am and asks me, "How was your night, Dad? How did you sleep? Where are you going today? What are you doing?" All the questions that little girls are supposed to ask their dad when he's getting ready in the morning.

After responding to each of her questions, I then ask her, "Megs, how are you doing?" Every morning for years, she's given me the exact same answer, "Awesome. I am awesome!"

Megan is someone who has dealt with enormous challenges already in her life. She still needs a ventilator to breathe and a wheelchair to get around. Thankfully, with the medicine we developed, we hope she will live many, many more decades and continue to get stronger.

For most people who don't know Megan and her story, "awesome" is probably not the adjective you'd pick to describe her situation.

But that's her optimism and it's not forced, it's genuine.

Part of being an optimist is never feeling sorry for yourself. That's a tough challenge to conquer. For anyone who has struggled, whether you're building a great university, a great business or a great life, it's easy to feel sorry for yourself when you continually get knocked down. But great entrepreneurs and great people know that feeling sorry for themselves won't help them achieve their goals, so they never let the thought enter their heads.

The fourth trait of great entrepreneurs is humility. Many of the most successful entrepreneurs I've met were humble. It's not easy in a world where people are constantly looking for their 15 minutes of fame. Most people want the recognition and press coverage for their achievements. But the great ones realize that fame is fleeting and it's not part of their core focus.

The company I run today, Amicus, came into existence because we thought there were new, innovative ways of treating human genetic disorders. The first three years were a magical, exciting time. The work we did culminated in an IPO.

We hit the big time! Every bank wanted to be part of the deal. They all told us how terrific we were and that great things were ahead for our company. We went on a road show in the spring of 2007. We traveled on a Gulfstream jet and sat in boardrooms filled with investors vying to get a piece of the deal. After two weeks on the road, our book was seven to eight times oversubscribed. Our company had a $300 million valuation and we raised $75 million dollars in capital. We approved the deal.

The morning after the deal went through, I brought the entire company with me to watch the trading at the Morgan Stanley desk in NYC. That afternoon we celebrated with a great lunch. Amicus had just created 12 millionaires. More important, we had the necessary capital to advance the programs that were important to us.

Needless to say, I felt pretty good about myself. I did an interview with CNBC and then closed the stock exchange. That night, my wife and I went home. As we checked on our sleeping kids, I went into Megan's room to give her a kiss goodnight. Still awake, she was excited to see me. She said, "I saw you on TV today." At this point, I'm thinking, I did pretty well these last couple of weeks. I looked at her and said, "Well Megan, it was a big couple of weeks for our company and our family." I said, "I think Daddy did pretty well this week. What do you think?" She replied, "I was so excited Daddy when I saw you on TV." I said, "Oh yeah, well how'd I look on TV?" She said, "Well, you looked really, really, really..." I'm thinking, *powerful, important*, pick the adjective. She continued, "Really short."

A little lesson in humility from my daughter. However, it also served as a reminder of what is important to me. As quickly as success comes, by the grace of God, it could be gone the next day. That night, standing next to Megan's bed, I realized that she wasn't very impressed with our IPO. She wasn't impressed with a big Gulfstream plane and she didn't even really care about Merrill Lynch or Morgan Stanley. What was important to her was having her dad home. She really missed me during those two weeks. She also thought about things like going to school the next day, and a friend's birthday party that weekend. That's what life, for me, is all about ... making sure my kids are happy and thinking about having fun and birthday parties.

I read an inspiring book several years ago by Anna Quindlen; it's called *A Short Guide to a Happy Life*. In her book, Anna says that, "Life is a terminal illness — we're all going to die from it. The measure of your life is how you live those days in between and how you spend your time."

It's a great lesson. As entrepreneurs, we work really hard. And hard work is often the price of success. But you need to find balance in life, too. It's still a constant struggle with me. It's something I tried to instill in the seniors at Princeton University. It's something I try to instill in my friends and colleagues. It's something I try to balance every day.

Geeta Anand, a Wall Street Journal reporter, spent a lot of time with our family. She wrote many articles, and then the book that inspired *Extraordinary Measures*. In the epilogue of her book, *The Cure*, Geeta wrote about putting the proper perspective on time and what it means to each of us in our lives:

As human beings we are defined at our cores by how we respond to hardship. Writing about the Crowleys has taught me that there is not one right way but that each person must find her own path, drawing on her own strength, passion, and resources. Who can say whether John or Eileen's role is more important? Fueled by love, each of their journeys is tough, vital, and courageous. Knowing that each day really may be their children's last, they live with abandon, throwing themselves into every birthday party, trips to Broadway, weekends at Ocean City, knowing so intimately the tenuousness of life. They instinctively understand what most of us sometimes forget: that all they really have and all they really are pursuing is time. Time with the people they love. So they grab onto each precious moment, cherish it, celebrate it, laugh at it, cry at it, and hope for another, even as they continue onto the journey into the unknown and the unknowable that we call life.

CHAPTER 9

Leveraging Collaboration for Innovation

Carlos Dominguez , senior vice president in the Office of the Chairman of the Board and CEO at Cisco

Carlos Dominguez

Carlos Dominguez presented at the Rothman Institute's Fourth Annual Innovation Summit on April 30, 2009. At the time he was a senior vice president in Cisco's Office of the Chairman of the Board and CEO. He advocates for the broad and creative use of technologies that are transforming how companies do business and creating distinct competitive advantages and new business models for those who adopt them.

He maintains that video, Web 2.0 applications and the use of social networks are at the heart of the collaboration revolution that is helping companies use the power of collective intelligence to produce revolutionary ideas for new products, better customer service and greater cost reductions.

Dominguez, who has been with Cisco for 17 years, has first-hand experience in how the company deploys technology in good, and bad, economic times to drive productivity and growth. He also advises Cisco customers about technology strategy and direction, spending time with start-up companies operating solely on the web as well as with established companies that are interested in using Internet innovations to do business differently.

As of spring 2010, Dominguez remains a senior vice president at Cisco.

Innovation is the introduction of something new. Whether it's a new product, service or way of doing something, innovation is about changing the status quo. Today, *everything* is changing. The way we do things at home, the way we communicate, the way we run our businesses and the way we conduct ourselves are all changing. We are moving to a more inclusive society where collaboration is preferred over doing things alone.

What is the catalyst for change? Most people will point to technology. We've come a long way in the last 20-30 years. It's much easier today to talk with people halfway around the world than it was just five years ago. However, technology is only one of the three pillars of our new, collaborative world. The other two pillars are process and culture. In today's business world, project teams cannot work on innovative programs without having the three pillars of collaboration firmly in place. They simply will not be successful.

In order to appreciate the rapidly changing role of collaboration in business, it's important to look back and gauge the historic increase in the speed of change:

- » The Internet is the fastest growing tool of communications ever.

- » 48% of all Internet users have been to video sharing websites.

- » Over 1 billion people access the Internet from their mobile phones.

- » In 2010, less than two dozen homes in the U.S. will generate more bandwidth than the entire Internet in 1995.

- » In 1984, the largest company in Silicon Valley was Velo-bind, a bookbinding business.

Today, social media is democratizing everything. It's no longer about who you know or how well connected you are. If you are talented with creative ideas, there are ways for you to contribute. As the role of traditional media continues to decline in the U.S., it is being replaced by social media. People are starting to listen to individuals about news. They are creating their own channels of receiving and distributing information. News has become a collaborative process.

In the past, people were confined to small economic roles. Talent and ideas were trapped unless you knew somebody. Knowledge, power and capital were limited to a privileged few in the business world, and consumers played passive roles when it came to mass produced products.

Today, we see a role reversal. Consumers are now driving the technology demand circle. It's no longer the world of PCs, networking, email and IP telephony, but rather instant messaging, mobility, blogs and wikis. After a decade of investment, consumer technology is changing behaviors which, in turn, fuels demand for new technologies. As Charles Darwin once said, *"It is not the strongest of the species that survives, or the most intelligent, but the one that is most responsive to change."*

Looking ahead, smart companies will realize that, when it comes to collaboration, they want to be as diverse as possible. Collaboration is all about people. Diverse and large groups of people are smarter than an elite few. They are also better at solving problems, fostering innovation, coming to wise decisions and even predicting the future.

In 1973, Sociologist Mark Grannovetter wrote: *"The strength of weak ties in the most efficient networks is that they link to the broadest range of information, knowledge and experience."* Strong ties, those relationships between people who work, live or play together, lead to a redundancy in ideas since members tend to think alike. Conversely, weak ties, relationships between members of different groups, lead to a diversity of ideas as they tie together separate modes of thought.

At Cisco, we've looked at collaboration from a work group perspective to determine how we can drive it throughout the various location of our company that may be cross functional in nature. How do we get financing, manufacturing, sales and service all talking to each other? In short, how do we bring a lot of smart individuals together to create a better outcome?

One example of successful mass collaboration is Goldcorp, a Canadian gold mining company. In the late 1990's, the company was on the verge of going out of business. It was acquired by a New York investment banker, but continued to struggle. The company spent a considerable amount of money running models on where to find gold, but kept coming up empty-handed.

Through a fortuitous meeting with Linux founder Linus Torvalds at the MIT Young Presidents Club, the banker learned about mass collaboration. Torvalds was building an operating system to compete with Microsoft, and he was doing it virtually through volunteers on an open network.

The investment banker decided to put all of his company's data, over 40 terabytes, online and hold the Goldcorp Challenge. It was a contest with prizes up to $675,000 for those people who could correctly identify sites that yielded gold. The contest received over 120 submissions with half of the sites already known to the company. However, approximately 60% of the sites previously unknown to Goldcorp yielded substantial amounts of gold. Today, Goldcorp is a multibillion dollar, profitable company.

The irony of their good fortune is that none of the successful submissions came from geologists. The winners were mathematicians, scientists in different disciplines of chemistry, engineers and college kids. The common thread among the winners is that they all looked at the opportunity through a different lens.

Leveraging collaboration for innovation has tremendous implications for the future. Don Tapscott, author of *Wikinomics: How Mass Collaboration Changes Everything*, wrote: *"A power shift is underway, and a tough business rule is emerging. Harness the new collaboration or perish. Those that fail to grasp this will find themselves ever more isolated."*

Instead of finding content, content will find you. Not only will content find you, it will know the content you need. Collaboration is more critical than ever. It holds the keys to: how we work, who we work with, when we work, where we work and what tools we use. We must collaborate in order to innovate.

CHAPTER 10

Building Innovative Partnerships to Heal the World

*by Amir Dossal, executive director of the
United Nations Office for Partnerships*

Amir Dossal

On September 16, 2009 Amir Dossal spoke at the Rothman Institute's Social Innovation & Entrepreneurship Conference, giving hindsight on the genesis and development of innovative partnerships and its importance in today's world economy.

At the time, Dossal was the Executive Director of the United Nations Office for Partnerships, where he guided the development of strategic alliances with governments, corporations, foundations and philanthropists in achieving the Millennium Development Goals. He has established strategic partnerships in a number of sectors, covering a variety of issues. Dossal is the UN's Representative for the administration of Ted Turner's $1 billion donation, covering 450+ programmes and projects in children's health; women and population; climate change; and biodiversity. This includes social investments of over $560 million from numerous other partners. He also oversees management of the UN Democracy Fund, which aims to strengthen institutions and enhance democratic governance.

As of fall 2010, Dossal launched a nonprofit initiative named the Global Partnerships Forum.

The crises facing the world, such as climate change and poverty, cannot be solved by nations alone. Given the current economic situation, the world's most pressing challenges have to be addressed by governments in collaboration with non-state partners. These issues require original and modern solutions that can best be achieved through collaborating with private sector and other partners with access to expertise and resources. Using entrepreneurial principles, these partnerships have enormous potential for helping solve the world's economic, ecological and social problems.

The United Nations Secretary General, Ban Ki-moon, has asked corporations "to advance universal principles within their spheres of influence." Private-sector companies are important partners in the UN's quest to achieve the Millennium Development Goals (MDGs) as well as other goals and agendas. Public-private partnerships offer new and creative solutions by pooling together expertise, resources and efforts, leading to sustainable solutions. As the executive director of the United Nations Office for Partnerships, I oversee the development of these strategic alliances with governments, corporations, foundations and philanthropists.

An example of a strategic partnership is Ted Turner's $1 billion donation, covering 450-plus programs and projects in children's health, women and population, climate change, and biodiversity. Since Turner's generous donation to the UN Foundation more than 10 years ago, we have seen an exponential growth in innovative partnerships between the UN, the private sector and civil society. I refer to this change as the "Turner Factor." The innovative solutions derived from these collaborations have utilized resources that were never available before to the United Nations and make the MDGs more realistic and achievable within the next five years.

Underlying this change is the trend away from traditional charitable giving toward "smart" philanthropy. Companies increasingly embrace the concept of corporate social responsibility, including it in their core business models. In smart philanthropy, the focus is more on sustainable wealth creation rather than on traditional, top-down monetary giving. As more private-sector companies now come to the United Nations in search for opportunities to collaborate, our engagement is promised on three essential principles to ensure the success of a public-private partnership: (1) socially responsible investment, (2) creativity and (3) quick and action-oriented response.

Socially responsible investment is an investment, monetary or otherwise, in an aspect of society that is struggling. Instead of writing a check and hoping the problem will go away, socially responsible investments are thoughtful and outcome-based, aimed at finding a sustainable solution. For example, Nestlé's Healthy Kids Global Program teaches adolescents in developing countries the importance of a well-balanced diet, exercise and healthy living. The program's goal is to double the amount of countries offering physical education programs by the end of 2011, hoping to combat the issues of malnourishment and obesity.

Nestlé also collaborates with the Abidjan Research and Development Centre in Cote d'Ivoire on developing rural areas in Africa. This partnership hopes to increase agricultural productivity and food safety by improving and developing local crops in the West African region. Nestlé is investing in the future of these countries through the Nestlé Prize in Creating Shared Value program. Every two years, the company pledges an award of $461,000 to individuals, NGOs or small enterprises that have developed innovative solutions in the following areas: nutritional deficiencies in regional diets, access to clean water and further progress in rural development. Nestlé uses its expertise in the areas of health and nutrition to develop long-term, sustainable solutions, empowering local communities.

Creativity is another key component of successful public-private partnerships. Donors have been turning toward new ways to give that typically require less monetary contribution and yield higher impact. The Peace and Sport Initiative is a good example of such collaboration. It promotes peace and development in areas afflicted with extreme poverty, social unrest and conflict by establishing locally based field projects promoting social unity and tolerance. Peace and Sport, in collaboration with the U.N. Office for Sport, Development and Peace as well as my office, has launched numerous creative partnerships. These partnerships provide platforms that inspire collaboration, respect, and a culture for understanding. By promoting sports, Peace and Sport brings people together, especially young people, allowing them to put their differences aside. Teammates feel an inherent bond and responsibility to one another, forging friendships and alliances that extend beyond the field. Peace and Sport has devised a creative solution for areas presented with conflict and unrest, operating successfully in many countries including Cote d'Ivoire, Burundi, Israel-Palestine, Timor-Leste and Colombia.

Quick and action-oriented response is especially important in post-disaster situations. In areas stricken by natural disaster or conflict, timely response is critical. The longer it takes for help to arrive, the deeper these areas fall into disarray. On Jan. 12, 2010, a massive earthquake struck Haiti, killing hundreds of thousands of people and destroying most of the country's infrastructure. The U.N. Office for Partnerships quickly facilitated response from the private sector, foundations, and civil society in support of U.N. disaster relief.

The Haiti Hope project is an example. The project is a joint initiative of the Inter-American Development Bank, the Coca-Cola Co. and the Haitian government. The five-year program, estimated to cost $7.5 million, aims to double the income of more than 25,000 mango farmers in Haiti by developing a sustainable mango industry. The initiative will raise the farmers' standard of living by giving them access to the international market and contributing to the long-term development and revitalization of Haiti. It is a wonderful example of what can be done when civil society, business and the public sector work together toward sustainable development. It is equally impressive that the project was conceived and developed in just a few weeks.

These innovative public-private partnerships serve as pioneering models on how the concerted, entrepreneurial efforts of the public sector, corporations and civil society can make a difference in the lives of people living in extreme poverty or distress.

CHAPTER 11

Entrepreneurship at Any Age

By Doris Drucker, Inventor and Author

Doris Drucker

Doris Drucker, MS'63, gave the Rothman Institute's Third Annual Female Entrepreneur Lecture on March 31, 2006. At the time she was the founder and CEO of RSQ Associates. She invented an electronic instrument that translates voice volume to warning lights on a console. The patented Visivox® system is used in college lecture halls, auditoriums and churches.

Armed with engineering diagrams and extensive research data, she spent several years preparing for the launch of her new RSQ Associates in 1996. She kicked off a national marketing initiative aimed at putting the product on the shelves everywhere.

Drucker is also an author. Two years ago she published a memoir, "Invent Radium or I'll Pull Your Hair." The book, described as "wryly comic" and as a work of "literary distinction" by *The Atlantic Monthly*, recounts her relationship with her iron-willed mother.

Drucker is the widow of famed business writer and management consultant Peter Drucker. As of spring 2010, a 90-plus-year-old Drucker travels extensively to continue and further the legacy of her late husband's work.

Entrepreneurship is a complex idea. My husband, Peter Drucker, wrote a book called *Innovation and Entrepreneurship*. In the book, he states that an entrepreneur has to be both an innovator and a developer; a marketer and a manager of change, so that his ideas will be integrated into society.

Unfortunately, few people have the ability to be both an inventor and a business manager. Thomas Edison was undoubtedly one of the greatest inventors. However, all of the businesses he started eventually failed. They didn't fail at the same time, but he never made the successful leap into entrepreneurship.

One of the common fallacies regarding inventors is that only "young" people can be successful inventors. How can an "old" person be a successful inventor when they are always looking back into the past? The brightest inventors look forward. They are opportunists with optimistic outlooks. This is certainly one of the requirements, but inventors can have this outlook at any age. There is a qualification for being inventor that does apply for older people. They must be in reasonably good physical and mental health. They must have to have a lot of energy, patience and perseverance, because it takes a long time until an invention is developed. They will need emotional support as well. There are many disappointments and frustrations when someone is developing an idea.

If you decide that entrepreneurship is for you, there are several critical points to remember. First, everything costs three times as much as you anticipated, and takes three times as long to happen. You will need financial support from someone who provides you with food and shelter for a year or two, until your business takes off. Even if you make a profit, you have to plow it back into the business. One caveat for older entrepreneurs is that you should not expect to have outside investors. Venture capitalists put their money in companies run by younger people with a greater life expectancy. Apart from that, anybody at any age, who is willing to take risks, can be an entrepreneur. Having a bright idea is very risky; it's a gamble. Some make it big, while others eke out an acceptable level of competence and gain.

Timing is everything for inventors and entrepreneurs. If your product initially fails, it could have as much to do with when you came out with it as anything else. Everyone thinks that Alexander Graham Bell invented the telephone, and everyone is wrong. Philip Reece, a German inventor, came up with the idea for the telephone ten years earlier, but people didn't think they needed it. A decade later, people recognized the value, and Alexander Graham Bell's version of the telephone was accepted. I had a similar experience in my life, and I could kick myself that I did not develop the idea. I invented a pulse rate meter which allows doctors to check pulse rate and blood pressure. I thought it would be of value if doctors and their patients had a device which measured pulse rate and blood pressure consistently over a period of time.

I invented a strap which recorded the different measurements from time to time. I showed my invention to a cardiologist who thought it was a great idea, but without a market. Our conversation took place just prior to the fitness craze in America. Today, people use similar products to the one I invented to check their vital stats every 15 minutes while working out. The products typically cost about $50 to purchase. I'm sorry that I did not pursue my idea. It might have been a success.

One idea which I did follow through on was something called the Visivox. My idea came from listening to my husband give his speeches. Peter was nearly deaf which meant he could not hear how loud he spoke because he wasn't getting the echo back. I used to sit in the last row during his speeches. When his voice dropped, I waved my arms to signal that he needed to speak louder. After attending enough lectures where I constantly waved my arms, I thought there must be a better way for a speaker to recognize the volume of his voice. I came up with an idea with enough specific details that I got to my first round of key decisions. At this stage, I had two options. I could have given my idea to a company to develop the product, or I could have gone into manufacturing myself.

In speaking with other companies, I knew that the outsourcing option was an unlikely one. Some companies wanted too much equity while others simply said no. I decided to go into manufacturing for myself. I found a retired electronic engineer by the name of Albee O'Brian. After a few meetings, we decided to go into business together. Albee calculated how much it would cost to produce our device, and how many units we would have to sell to become profitable. Thankfully, he was quite accurate.

One thing I didn't realize as a manufacturer was how many "little" decisions are made in the process. For example, should the box be made out of plastic or metal? Should it have the lid? What about the dimensions of the box?

Albee made a list of the 70-80 parts we needed. Instead of buying directly from the manufacturers, where they usually sold lots in the tens of thousands, I took the list to all the discount houses. Eventually, after I got everything we needed in the quantities we needed, the next step was finding an assembler. I thought we were almost ready to go into production. Far from it. Once I found an assembler, he informed me that I would need separate people to do the circuit boards and layouts.

Finally, after getting the parts and finding the right people, we built five samples with 100 more on the way. We painted the boxes ourselves and showed them to many potential buyers. We were encouraged by some early orders and decided to order 100 more.

A bigger order could only mean one thing: bigger problems. The boxes needed to be spray painted. However, the manufacturer did not allow enough clearance for the hinges to be painted. The boxes didn't close. When we took the order back to the manufacturer, he was furious, and swore he'd never work with us again. After some back and forth discussions, we had our boxes.

We knew that our core target market was professional speakers. However, the market wasn't big enough for our product, so we decided to do some market research. Business companies seemed to be a good market for us. They wanted to use the Visivox in training seminars to teach salesmen how to speak at a consistent volume. We then tapped into other, non-core markets. Churches and speech pathologists became key markets for us.

When I stand back and think about all the difficulties and sleepless nights in creating the Visivox, I ask myself if I would start a business again. The answer is yes! I enjoy the entertainment of being both an inventor and an entrepreneur. I find it very rewarding to see my ambition and ingenuity rewarded, even in a modest way.

CHAPTER 12

Securing Relationships One at a Time

An interview with Kurus Elavia,
CEO, Gateway Group One

Kurus Elavia

Kurus Elavia sat down to talk with James Barrood in spring 2008 as part of the "Voices of Innovation" television series. At the time, he was CEO of Gateway Group One, a company he started working for in 1988 as a security guard. He steadily worked his way up the ranks to CEO, providing and executing the strategic planning that resulted in growing Gateway to nearly 4,000 employees and $70 million in revenues.

Elavia was named one of the *NJBIZ's* "40 under 40" business leaders in 2004. In 2006 he was given the Asian American Leadership Award by the Asian American Association for Human Services. He is a member of the American Association of Airport Executives Training and Diversity Board.

Gateway delivers premium security and frontline services to the region's three major airports and largest health-care facilities and many Fortune 50 companies. The company is known for its customer service and recruitment, training and retention of its employees. It was recognized as the "Fastest Growing Urban Company" for three consecutive years by *Inc.* Magazine.

As of spring 2010, Elavia remains CEO of Gateway and continues to lead the company's global expansion.

James Barrood: Kurus, I know you understand the role of innovation as well as any business leader. As a non-family employee, you run one of the fastest growing family businesses in the country. First, tell us how you went from entry-level security guard to CEO in just 19 years.

Kurus Elavia: My story is *our* story. It is truly an American dream. I applied at Gateway Group One as a security officer. I made $6.50 an hour starting on the loading dock. I then moved through the ranks of supervisor, assistant manager, manager and troubleshooter. One of my jobs was to go to sites that had issues with customer service delivery. My job was to make the customer smile again.

In 1999, I thought Gateway had a subconscious brand. The customers loved us, and there was tremendous potential, but we weren't recognized in the marketplace. I, along with one of the founders, created a business plan, and approached the ownership with the idea that we could double the business in three years. In return, they needed to trust us and give us access to the current infrastructure at the company.

When we started on this "fearless warrior" sort of journey, there were many parts of the plan that were unknowns. But, we knew that Gateway Group One offered the best service in our market. I became COO of the company and spent the next three years tripling our business. We went from 500 to almost 2,000 employees and made the *Inc. 500* list all three years.

Barrood: What does the word "innovation" mean to you?

Elavia: In my business, innovation can be found in the daily services we provide to our clients. Gateway is not creating a product in a separate facility and then shipping it to customers. We are manufacturing as we are delivering. Whether it's my customer service rep at the airport or my officer protecting a facility, they are providing a service. They are managing a thousand points of human touch and human delivery every single day. There is no one scientific method to our business. We work to achieve "trust-based" relationships. Our front line clearly determines the bottom line. So for us, innovation is about managing those thousand points of service delivery daily.

Barrood: When you come up with an innovative idea for your company, what do you do with it? Is there a formal process in developing innovative solutions at Gateway?

Elavia: Most of our ideas come from interacting with our clients. The voice of the customer plays a very important role in the success of this enterprise. In 1999, the Port Authority asked us to create a pilot service program called *Red Jacket*. They thought some airport customers wanted world-class service and experience, rather than just going to the airport, getting on a plane and leaving. We created a nine-member team to help launch the program. Today, it is one of the largest Port Authority service programs. We have over 500 staff members working at JFK, LaGuardia, and Newark airports, and have received several customer service awards for the program.

Barrood: Gateway Group One is a family business. Talk about how difficult it can be to bring new ideas or change into a family-run business.

Elavia: In our company, we have always viewed *family* as a relationship. Our mission statement, first written almost 28 years ago, was *"securing relationships one at a time."* We believe that trust-based relationships are the cornerstones of a family-member relationship, of an employee-employee relationship, of a customer-employee relationship, and a business-partner relationship.

The family behind Gateway is a big part of the fabric of this organization. They have strong relationships with not only me, but also with the rest of the team. Our turnover rate is very low. Thankfully, many of the issues and obstacles that you find in a typical family-run business don't exist with us. This type of relationship breeds motivation, innovation and success. It makes everyone work harder. Our customer retention is 98%. The first five customers that helped create Gateway Security are still with us.

Barrood: With 4,000 employees today, how do you lead and foster innovation among the employees? How do you keep everyone actively involved in the business?

Elavia: In a service business, it's all about human potential. Everyone must feel as if they have a role in the success of our company. We recruit the best people for our team. We get them excited to be part of Gateway. We provide them with solid, practical training. We forge a trust-based relationship with our employees and then we send them out into the marketplace to represent us.

Barrood: Most other businesses have huge turnover rates, particularly in this industry. What's your secret?

Elavia: It's good old-fashioned hard work. We are blessed to have a diverse workforce which is a big advantage for us. At the airports, we were one of the first companies to have a bilingual staff. This advantage empowered our employees. They believed their diversity was critical in our success. We give them an 800 number to call with compliments or to air their grievances. There's also a 24/7 hotline for our employees. We want them to know that we support them and stand behind them when they need us. We also provide better benefits than our competitors. The employees at Gateway don't feel like it's a job to them, they see our company as their career. That's the secret.

Barrood: In speaking about innovation & diversity, research shows that the more diverse the team or company, the better the product or service. Innovation clearly thrives in diverse settings. Can you elaborate on that point?

Elavia: A lot of companies use diversity as a sound bite. We are a diverse company. If I took a world map and put pins indicating where my employees came from, the entire map would be filled up. We use our diversity as an asset because everyone brings a different view to the business. We nurture and encourage diversity. There is another side to diversity, and that is divisiveness. We will never allow someone to use our different backgrounds to divide our company. We foster a free-thinking, "we're all on the same team" type of culture in our company. When discussing a project or opportunity, anyone can weigh in with their ideas. We look at all of them and then decide on an execution strategy. A great, innovative idea without a proper execution strategy is just that... an idea. We empower employees to develop the execution strategy as well. They take total ownership and we provide their support.

Barrood: What about failure? When we speak about innovation, we speak about failure as a critical part -- learning from that experience and applying it the next time around.

Elavia: Failure occurs only when we stop trying. We have not experienced failure in our minds, because we have not given up.

Yes, we hit bumps in the road. We don't win all the contracts, but that doesn't mean we stop bidding on work. We learned from the bumps so that we don't hit the same bumps again. We refine our strategy and change the method of implementation for the next time. We know we won't win every time, but we do expect to win our fair share of business.

Barrood: Do employees feel that they can test new ideas, concepts and programs without worrying that failure might cost them their jobs?

Elavia: We don't have a strict policy of "one-and-done" in our company. We will keep trying as long as we believe we're on the right road. It's taken Gateway 28 years to get to where we are now, and it hasn't been one easy, straight path. We've had our growing pains. But, in an industry where the turnover rate is 300%, and where large firms are buying up the smaller players, Gateway has managed to grow organically while remaining in Newark. And, in an industry that has 30-day termination clauses written into almost every contract, we've held onto clients for over 20 years! That is a testament to our entire team. It starts with the inspired vision of ownership, and then works its way through my executive staff, my management staff and our employees.

Barrood: Most companies today are service-based businesses. What insight or advice would you give to people running these companies to help them grow their businesses and be more innovative?

Elavia: First, **listen to your customers.** Never stop asking them, "How can I make it better for you?" Second, **don't make promises that you can't keep.** The experience and the expectation model must work. If the expectations aren't met with the experience, at some point, there is a degradation of service. Once that happens, it's very difficult to rebound. You have broken the trust-based relationship. Third, **always be in tune with your employees.** They are the mechanisms of service delivery. No matter how well a product is made, it is ultimately delivered by the employees of your company.

Barrood: What about recent graduates and people working at larger companies--how can they improve their creativity or innovative skills and add more value to their organization?

Elavia: They can improve their creative and innovative skills by asking two simple questions: First, why do we do things this way? And second, how can I make something better? Then, they must be ready to be a part of the solution. It's great to ask questions, but if you are the author of the question, we expect you to be author of the answer as well. If you do not have an answer, someone else will.

Throughout history, some of the greatest ideas and inventions never turned into innovations for the inventors. Someone else came along, took the idea and executed it. For recent graduates and people working at larger organizations, it's important to follow through on your work. Try to maintain ownership of the idea or concept. No one understands it quite like the person who came up with it.

CHAPTER 13

How I Quit Treading Water and Learned to Swim

By Seth Gerszberg, CEO of Marc Ecko Enterprises

Seth Gerszberg

Seth Gerszberg gave the Rothman Institute's Seventh Annual Richard M. Clarke Distinguished Entrepreneurial Lecture on May 5, 2005. At the time, he was president of Marc Ecko Enterprises. He, along with Head Designer Marc Ecko and Executive Vice President Marci Tapper, founded *ecko unltd. in 1993 as a graffiti-inspired T-shirt company. They were honored in 2001 with the E&Y Entrepreneur of the Year Award. With an insatiable appetite for success and ability to learn, Gerszberg has turned a modest T-shirt company into a $1 billion clothing and lifestyle empire.

*ecko unltd. continues to transcend the boundaries of traditional business with interests ranging from clothing to video game design and production. With over 12 distinct lines of fashion and accessories, the company also publishes a bimonthly urban and street-culture magazine, *Complex*.

As of spring 2010, Gerszberg holds the position of chief executive officer of Marc Ecko Enterprises and is responsible for business development and strategic planning, in addition to directing MEE's marketing and creative services, brand imaging, licensing, international development, and MEE's retail growth strategy.

In 1993, I gave a young man named Marc Ecko $55,000 to start a T-shirt company. Marc was 20 years old at the time and made 5,000 shirts. He sold them for $10 apiece and we lost $5,000. I realized that he needed help, so I became his partner. We spent the next six years, through 1999, losing $6 million.

The first thing we did was identify a customer base that was previously unknown to us. In 1993, Marc was a white Jewish kid, living in Lakewood, New Jersey and listening to hip hop music. He didn't know any other white Jewish kids in Lakewood that listened to hip hop. His interests were graffiti, sports and hip hop. He thought to himself, "There must be other kids like me."

My background was somewhat similar in that I was Orthodox Jewish, living in Lakewood and I loved sports. However, I didn't know Marc, didn't go to public school and didn't listen to hip hop. Still, when we met, we decided that there must be a market or an opportunity to find more people like us.

We made clothes that white kids could wear, black kids could wear, white kids who liked black kids could wear and black kids who liked white kids could wear. All the black stores said, "*You can't be serious. That is way too white.*" All the skate stores said, "*That's way too black.*" In a nutshell, nobody wanted to buy it. We decided to give all the goods away on consignment, the lowest form of commerce in this country. Consignment is like begging; it's saying "please take my stuff. It's so bad that I can't even sell it to you."

Surprisingly, most of our clothes sold on consignment. Stores then paid us and asked for more pieces to sell. After some initial success, Marc came to me one day and said, "*Seth, we can't be a novelty T-shirt company anymore. We really need to make clothes.*" That was the worst day in my life. I didn't know it then, but I am telling you the story in retrospect, and it was the worst day of my life.

I heard that they made jeans in California, so I went there. I opened the Yellow Pages and found a jeans maker. I gave him a 50% deposit and I waited. I waited and then waited some more. Do you know what happens when someone is two months late with 50 percent of your money and they are ready to ship to you? You pay them 100% on what is left and say, "Thank you." That's what we did. We got the jeans and shipped them out quickly without taking the time to inspect them. We immediately started getting calls because the buttons popped off as soon as people tried on the jeans.

We then found a rivet company in Tennessee that agreed to put rivets on our jeans. Two weeks later — after promising me they would be ready in two days— I flew down to Tennessee to meet with my rivet partner. It was a husband and wife team manually putting the rivets on jeans in their garage. It was some sight. The good news was that the rivets stayed on and our customers got their jeans back.

The first lesson in business is to have a purpose for being. Your company needs a reason to exist. Identify an opportunity that no one else has found, and approach it with a unique, entrepreneurial spirit. If you are right, you will be rewarded for your efforts.

The second lesson in business is that a great idea does not a business make. Having an idea without having the means to successfully execute it means absolutely nothing. It will remain just an idea. We found that, if we had the right product, the right marketing at the right time of year, in the right trade show, with the right mindset and a crossover customer that nobody's ever identified, that we could write $4 million worth of orders in three and half days. That's exactly what happened. We quickly found a new manufacturer in Taiwan that agreed to design, market, sell and ship all of our clothing.

The relationship started off on a strong note, but it was a very short honeymoon. In the spring of 1997 our manufacturer missed their shipment. We promised our customers that their clothes would arrive in January. It was the end of February and they still had no clothes.

We went to a trade show, and the same customers believed in us enough to place more orders. We took in $7.3 million worth of orders at the show. There was one problem. The initial $4.3 million in orders never came. What we did get was $2.1 million worth of orders, half of which were shippable. The other half of our order was made in the worst factories in China. There were oil stains from faulty sewing machines that splattered all over the knits that we made. In addition, many boxes that were marked 36 pieces only had 24 items inside of them.

We needed another partner. We needed someone who knew what they were doing when it came to manufacturing. Surprisingly, we found a lot of clothing companies interested in being our partner. Levi's, Ralph Lauren, Nautica, and Perry Ellis, to name a few, were all interested in partnering with us. It was surreal as each of these very successful companies wanted to buy us. That is, until they looked at our books. We had $6 million in debt and $15 million in sales. Suddenly, the wooing stopped and all the successful companies walked away. But, they left behind some valuable lessons for us. Nautica taught us about planning, Polo taught us about marketing, and Perry Ellis showed us how to properly forecast our business. It was only going through the process of trying to sell our company that we learned how to correctly run it.

I tried very hard to sell the company. At that time, I would have given 100% of the company, with me as an indentured servant, if they assumed our debt. The problem was that most our debt came from friends, family and fools. We were good salesmen in making our loved ones believe in us. They gave us their money and all I wanted to do was pay it back.

The third lesson in business is that money is not always the answer to every problem. When we had no money, it meant we had to be creative in order to achieve our goals. In my mind, it was the best thing that ever happened to us. We did many things in our company's history where we competed on ideas and not on dollars. When we looked at running a commercial during the Super Bowl, we found out it was $2 million. Then, we called Spike Lee about shooting a commercial. We wanted to have rhinos running down Madison Avenue, and all the fashion houses would crumble under the weight of the rhinos. It would signal the dawn of a new day, and we were the new fashion house. We asked Spike about the cost. He simply said: "Millions and millions and millions!" So we decided to find another way.

We did some research on the Macy's Thanksgiving Day parade and found out that 52 million people watched it last year. A float in the parade that year cost $250,000 and would be $125,000 for the following two consecutive years. We eventually got "Rhino Mountain" in the Thanksgiving Day parade. We also got 52 million impressions for the cost of $250,000. Not too bad.

Our biggest creditor during this period was my cousin. He had an apparel business in Houston, and lent us $3 million. I explained to him that I had a verbal agreement with a licensing company. With his money, we could pay immediate creditors, get our licensing revenue and help pay back the $6 million to friends and family. The licensing company was going to make all of our clothes. We would help them market the product lines and receive a royalty. I can still remember getting the call from the company. It was a Tuesday, and the gentleman on the other end of the line said, *"We won't be able to do the deal."*

I was 26 years old with $6 million in debt. I had a wife and two kids, living in a rent-stabilized apartment. My partners didn't know what was happening, and all of our credit cards were maxed out. Every day, I came into the office trying to sell the company. I thought it was a done deal with the licensing company. When they said, "No," I could feel my heart begin to pound very quickly. I started to sweat, and then passed out on the floor. When my assistant walked in and found me like a chalk outline on the floor, she started to yell. All hell broke loose, and I realized that I might actually die. I got up, picked up the phone and called up my cousin. I told him *"I got a problem which just might kill me, and if I die, you will never get back your $3 million."*

He and I talked about my business. I needed help getting out of our deep hole of debt. I wasn't a sophisticated financier, and I didn't want to deal with the multiple on earnings. I asked him *"How much in ownership, in exchange for a loan that we will pay off, could I give you for this company that I love very much, but I can't afford to run right now?"* My cousin was incredibly generous. He gave us very favorable terms which stretched out over a five-year period. More importantly, he gave us a million and a half dollars.

We were back in business. Now, we could answer the phones without worrying whether it was a customer or a bill collector. We could actually sell our products, and we had received a great education when Ralph Lauren and all the other companies initially tried to buy us. We took our new-found education and the ability to tread water, and we started swimming. We took the $1.5 million and paid down the most immediate of our debts. We became incredibly focused. In 1999, we went from $15 million in sales to $36 million in sales.

In the first six months of 2000, we did another $36 million in sales, and we had bookings for $60 million over the next six months. More importantly, we were profitable. We paid back my cousin, and my cousin gave us back our 70 percent stake in the company.

Our story is one of perseverance and learning from our mistakes. It's also about giving back. In January, 1999, I heard about a struggling orphanage in the Ukraine. At that time, we were probably struggling even more. I said to my partners, *"If we ever get out of this mess, pay back our debt and win back our company, let's commit the first $100,000 of our profit to this charity."*

In October, 2000, I had the good fortune of going to Odessa, Ukraine to visit the orphanage. Since then, we have partnered with another group to help run the organization. We have doubled its size so that we can provide assistance to even more children in the Ukraine. We also run corporate citizenship programs, such as Sweat Equity Enterprises, which educates young, underprivileged children in the areas of design, development and other business opportunities.

The last lesson in business for today is to focus on others first. When you develop your business plan, start with understanding that you're dealing with real people who have real ambitions, desires and goals. If you come to them and offer solutions to their problems and their needs, you will be rewarded tenfold. However, if you start your business plan with how to fulfill your own needs first, you won't get very far. You need to give, in order to get.

CHAPTER 14

Nurturing Innovation in Small Businesses

*An interview with Leonard Green, founder
and president of The Green Group*

Leonard Green

Leonard Green sat down to talk with James Barrood in spring 2008 as part of the "Voices of Innovation" television series. At the time, he was president and founder of The Green Group, a tax and financial services consulting firm. He is an owner or investor in more than a dozen different businesses, encompassing real estate, thoroughbred horses, and a sports team.

At Babson College, Green teaches a course structured similarly to Donald Trump's "Apprentice" television series and an entrepreneurial family business course. His classes have been featured on CNBC "Squawk Box" and ABC-TV. He has also taught entrepreneurship courses at Fairleigh Dickinson University. His articles on family business, succession planning and his courses have appeared in over 200 newspapers, including the *Wall Street Journal*, *New York Post*, and *Inc.* Magazine.

Green is on the advisory board of many family-owned businesses and consults with over 1,000 clients. He is on the board of NYSE-listed Cenveo Inc. and several nonprofits.

As of spring 2010, Green remains the head of his family business and continues to motivate his team to launch new ventures on a regular basis.

James Barrood: Len, as a successful entrepreneur, the head of one of the most dynamic family businesses in the country, a consultant to hundreds of family firms and as a very popular business professor, the experience and wisdom you have gained over the years is impressive. Whenever I hear you speak, I always learn something new. Len, tell us about your entrepreneurial journeys.

Len Green: It's amazing, looking back over the years, how many people assumed that I had no chance of being successful. I graduated near the bottom part of my high school class, and about the same spot in college. In addition, I was fired from my first seven jobs. These are not achievements that most people would relate with success. But, it's important to note that people not only mature at different times, they also find their passion at different times. It's finding that passion that is the difference between success and failure in the world. When I teach, I always ask my students what section of the paper do they read first. If they had to pick two or three things that they really enjoyed doing, never mind whether they could make a living of it, what would they do? Once a person finds something they love to do, the next step is to gain enough knowledge to do something in that field. The last step is to find a problem out there that's not being solved or that you can solve better than somebody else. At this point, the whole world opens up.

Barrood: It's interesting to follow your path, from college graduate to serial entrepreneur. Tell us about your personal journey.

Green: I think you have to start at the lowest point first. Believe it or not, the lowest point was not getting fired from seven jobs. It was when my Air Force unit got activated into active duty and suddenly, I found myself taking orders. There was no innovation, and nobody wanted to change things. I worked in 100 degree weather with no air conditioning. I got to a point where I thought, "There must be a better way." For me, it was buying a $1.95 J.K. Lasser tax book. I became the tax guru of the base, and prepared everyone's tax returns.

When I was discharged from the Air Force, I decided to go back to school and get a graduate degree in taxation. The first day in class, the professor asked if a certain expense was deductible. I shot my hand up and , "Yes, it is." He asked: "What's your source?" I said, "J.K. Lasser's tax book." Everyone in the class laughed. They were talking about case law and regulations, codes and private rulings. I had no idea what I was doing. I thought I could go to graduate school for taxation because I enjoyed it so much and because I had memorized a book. I knew what was deductible and what was an income. The professor figuratively gave me a dime and told me to make a telephone call. I wasn't going to make it.

I went home and told my wife the story. I couldn't hack graduate school because these other students were all from large law firms and accounting firms. They talked in a foreign language. My wife's reply was classic. She said, "I guess you can't hack it, Len." I knew right then that she was testing me. I could hack it. I went back to school and graduated number one in my class. After graduate school, I landed with a national firm, which gave me exposure to many smart people. I worked my way up the ladder, but realized that, as much as I loved taxes, I loved business entrepreneurship even more. When the opportunity arose, I passed on becoming a partner in the firm and started all over again. I remember coming home and saying, "Lois, I just bought a shopping center, we're $4 million in debt and I have no job." She replied, "I'm pregnant." Talk about a motivating reason to succeed!

I had the opportunity to take some calculated risks, which I did, and things worked out very well.

Barrood: Let's fast-forward to today.

Green: Today, I love sitting on advisory boards, and I love to teach. I remember a conversation that took place on one of my boards that focused on the energy drink market. After some back and forth between the 20 year-olds and the 40-50 year-olds, we came up with an idea for an energy drink that would target people going to the X-games and other similar events. It was SoBe.

Another board conversation centered on holistic dog and cat food. We read an article about a doctor that had developed a formula that reduced cancer in animals by 75% when you mixed it with their food. We knew PetSmart was looking for a new, holistic line of healthy dog food/cat food, so we suggested that we buy the doctor's formula and start a new line of pet food. We called PetSmart and made a presentation. They placed an order for one million SKUs. I told my wife, "Lois, I just got an order for a million SKUs." She shook her head and replied, "You have no product, no manufacturer, and no label." I said, "Yeah, but we got an order for a million SKUs and we know we can make the best dog food and cat food."

Barrood: Let's talk about taking an opportunity from idea to reality. You've successfully launched many businesses. How does innovation play a role in your launches or re-launches?

Green: Innovation is thinking differently than other people think. If you do things the way they've always been done or the way other companies do it, you will just be ordinary. Companies fail because they don't use innovation or reinvent themselves. They don't listen to the customers, and they don't use change to motivate the people around them. I have a great team. I couldn't run different companies without having a great team. When I meet with my team, we discuss different strategies, and we get input from everyone. Agreement is critical because I then tie their compensation to the results of the agreed upon strategies. I empower my team. In turn, they empower their management teams. Everyone becomes an owner of their specific plan. We encourage them to take calculated risks and to come up with new ideas or new ways to get the desired results. To me, this is promoting innovation and reinvention throughout my companies.

Barrood: If one of your employees comes up with an idea, what is the process of taking that idea from conception to reality in one of your companies?

Green: When an employee has a good idea for one of our companies, they call a hotline and explain their idea. Once a month, a group meets to discuss the hotline ideas. We never dismiss any idea. If we can't see value in an idea, we ask the employee to flesh it out for us. Obviously, they see something that we don't see. We view hotline ideas as a viable program to keep us a step or two ahead of the bigger companies. A smaller company, lean and mean, that works fast and effectively, can outdo the dinosaurs every day of the week. Our hotline program is one example of us staying ahead of the dinosaurs.

Barrood: You've taken a company with a few employees to one with many employees. How did you make the transition from sole proprietor to a successful, growing mid-sized company?

Green: I'm fortunate in that I know I can't run companies. I turn the running of a company over to people who know what they are doing. Then I motivate them by getting them to commit to certain goals and objectives. Once I have the goals and objectives in place, I put together a compensation plan for them. In my businesses, we ask people if they want stock or cash. At certain stages, they need to have cash (raising kids, buying homes). At other times, they agree to either a combination plan or just stock.

Barrood: Let's switch gears a little and talk about family-run businesses. You have one. Tell us about the different dynamics in family businesses versus regular small businesses.

Green: In most companies, the top motive is profit. In a family business, it's mainly about the quality of the product. Our name is connected with the business. We also worry about succession plans. Who are the next generation of leaders? Does it have to be family members?

I remember coming home from Harvard and going into my dad's business. I had some new ideas about hors d'oeuvres and other fancy items. He said, "We've been in business since 1865, selling the same things over and over. It's worked for several generations. Why don't you think it's going to work for your generation?" I replied, "Dad, times are changing. We need to keep pace." We compromised!

Barrood: How do you manage change if you're not the founder of the business?

Green: It's tough. There's a big shadow for the person following the founder as the leader of a company. When I asked my kids which companies of ours they wanted to run, they said, "None of them." I then asked them to come up with an idea of a company that they wanted to run, and how it would fit under our umbrella of companies. So they did. Since then, they've had a chance to prove their worth as founders of their own companies while gaining valuable experience. They also earned the respect of their colleagues and co-workers, not just as the son or daughter of the company founder, but as someone who built up their own business.

Barrood: If one of your children has an idea and that idea doesn't go anywhere, at least they know they've been heard, correct? Should we assume it goes through a process just like any other idea from one of your employees?

Green: That's correct. Their ideas are judged exactly the same as every other idea. I strongly suggest that all family businesses set up advisory boards. But, it can't be their accountant, their lawyer or their banker. Instead, have successful people who know nothing about your businesses. Yet, they need to be smart enough to ask the right questions and motivate the employees.

Barrood: You have talked about failure within your companies and not wanting to penalize any employees too harshly. Can you expand on that philosophy and provide an example?

Green: To me, you learn more from failures than you do from successes. The question then becomes *how do you view failures?* Is failure a failure? Or, is failure an opportunity to look at something, re-examine it, see what went wrong, and then figure out how to profit from the original failure? I believe that, if we're not failing as a company, then we're not going to succeed. It means we're not trying hard enough, and we're not trying new things.

I told you about the great success story about our dog food/ cat food business. It's now up to $15 million a month in sales. The same day that we started that company, we launched two other companies. One company created a drink to rival Red Bull. We had all the distributors in place and we knew the business because of our success with SoBe. The second company had a product that dealt with ulcers in horses. As a horse owner, I'm pretty knowledgeable about the business and the industry. I have over 100 horses and have won 1,200 races. So we start three companies on the same day. Two companies look like sure things. We have the background, the expertise and the distribution channels in place. Which company succeeded? The dog and cat food business; the one we knew nothing about.

Were the first two companies failures? No. They simply reinforced the fact that you can't just do the same thing over and over again. The marketplace changes. Entrepreneurship is a learning process.

Barrood: Whether you are an entrepreneur or an innovator, how important is passion for your business idea? Are there times when passion is not enough?

Green: Entrepreneurs and innovators need to look at their ideas and make sure there is a void in the marketplace for their product or service.

I was amazed when Pepsi paid $370 million to buy SoBe. Why didn't they just start the business themselves? They didn't visualize the potential of the market. Big dinosaurs get into a box where they cannot see outside the four walls. They also don't want to take as many calculated risks as a start-up company.

People constantly ask me for advice and tips for success. I

tell them, "Kenny Rogers said it best when he said, 'Know when to hold 'em, and know when to fold 'em.' " Just as I tell people to not lose faith in themselves and their ideas, they shouldn't be afraid to end a project or program that isn't working and move on to something else.

CHAPTER 15

Customer Focus –
A Prescription for Driving Innovation

*By Fred Hassan, a senior advisor with
Warburg Pincus, and former chairman and
CEO of Schering-Plough*

Fred Hassan

Fred Hassan gave the Rothman Institute's Inaugural CEO Innovation Lecture on February 23, 2006. At the time he was chairman and chief executive officer of Schering-Plough Corporation. Those positions were the latest in a 30-year career committed to fostering innovation and science-centered entrepreneurship in the pharmaceutical industry. Hassan has a strong track record of executing transformational change in complex global companies. His leadership approach includes a deep focus on fostering attitudes and behaviors among colleagues that are critical to driving long-term high performance — including collaboration, shared accountability and listening and learning.

Prior to joining Schering-Plough in April 2003, Hassan was chairman and chief executive officer of Pharmacia Corporation. He was executive vice president and a director of Wyeth, formerly American Home Products. He also spent 17 years with Sandoz (now Novartis).

As of spring 2010, Hassan is a senior advisor with Warburg Pincus, a private equity firm. In 2009, he stepped down from Schering-Plough following the merger with Merck.

Innovation is in our genes. When talking about innovation, we must remember that it is central to the strength, growth and vitality of people, of organizations and of society itself. In taking a closer look at the topic, three key questions come to mind. First, *what exactly is innovation, and why is customer focus so important to innovation?* Second, *what makes innovation happen?* And third, *what needs to be done to sustain innovation?*

Innovation and the Importance of Customer Focus

Thomas Edison once asked, "Is there a way to do it *better?*" He then added, "If so, find it!" Edison's point is succinct but deep. He is telling us that innovation is not just great thinking or great creativity in a vacuum. It is creativity that is active, that delivers something new and better. It also implies new and better for a purpose that adds value.

We should think of innovation as creativity in action, or *applied creativity.* Applied creativity creates something new or better, while adding value for individuals or for society. We don't know who invented it, but the wheel did not change civilization simply because of the creative genius that went into the discovery. The wheel was a profound innovation because it was *applied.* The application of the wheel for transportation, and thousands of other needs, transformed human life for the better.

This formula exists in every real innovation. Some innovations radically changed the world -- the steam engine, the telephone, the automobile, the airplane and the microchip. Other innovations added value in smaller ways, such as power steering, synthetic clothing fabrics, the zipper and the iPod.

I found one example of applied creativity while reading an article in *Nature* magazine. According to the article, U.S. soldiers serving in

Iraq, and on other missions, did not always have access to toothbrushes and floss. Approximately 15% of soldiers reported that they were suffering from toothaches and gum disease. In response to this need, researchers identified a protein fragment called KSL. The protein fragment eats holes in the cell membranes of the bacteria that cause dental disease and kills them. The researchers then figured out how to embed KSL in chewing gum. The chewing gum formulation turned the creativity of the KSL discovery into a solution for soldiers and others who can't brush or floss. According to Patrik DeLuca, one of the researchers who invented the new chewing gum, the innovation is valuable "not only for the military, but also for the avid outdoorsman and anyone else on the go."

The research-based pharmaceutical industry is a special example of innovation. At its essence, we transform great science into treatments that improve and save people's lives. The complex work begins in a science laboratory with basic research by talented scientists who discover new chemical compounds and new molecules.

However, to turn scientific creativity into an innovation, we engage thousands of other people in highly complex and costly actions. These actions transform a molecule into a treatment – with continuous applications of further creativity. This form of applied creativity produces something new or better to improve health.

One of the best ways to think about the beneficiary of innovation is to think about the customer. In broad terms, the customer is someone to whom you deliver added value. In most cases, the customer is a person, organization or society with a need that will be met by your innovation. Focusing on the customer thus becomes a way of figuring out how to make innovation happen.

Consider a recent innovation – Apple's iPod. It responds to the desire of consumers for personal, portable and flexible music. It takes the creative technology of storing music electronically and applies it, with further creativity, into a new consumer electronic device. The iPod has transformed the way people listen to music, how they share music and how they socialize.

The iPod is a great example of the power of customer focus. By being in tune with its customers and sensing an unmet need, Apple applied its creativity to add value. Innovation does not happen in a vacuum or inside a closed system. Scientists and technicians could labor for decades over the same electronics that are inside an iPod and never produce this type of spectacular consumer breakthrough. It was customer focus that was the prescription for the innovation.

The iPod example illustrates another important dimension of innovation. In the 17th century, Sir Isaac Newton said, "*If I have seen further, it is by standing upon the shoulders of giants.*" In essence, Newton benefited from the foundation work created by others. Most innovation builds on the other advances before them. Even breakthrough innovations are a result of "*building on the shoulders of giants.*" When you look at the iPod, it benefited from the work of old fashioned tape players, microchip advances, Sony Walkmans and many others devices.

In medicine, every breakthrough has a family tree of earlier successes. One example is the treatment of cardiovascular disease and high cholesterol, one of the biggest killer diseases in the world. Our industry has created very effective breakthrough treatments for high cholesterol. They are responses to a very serious need of the ultimate customer – the patient.

The incremental innovations that preceded these treatments go back decades. The first so-called "statin" molecule was discovered in the early 1970's. Scientists built on that knowledge and created the first synthetic statin molecules. In 1987, Merck brought out Mevacor, the first, widely available statin. Other statin treatments, such as Lipitor, followed Mevacor and the innovation continued.

Schering-Plough discovered Ezetimibe, a completely new molecule that attacks cholesterol through a new mechanism of action. The medicine has created a new paradigm for treating cholesterol.

Another dimension of customer focus with enormous importance is customer service. In many ways, customer service is process innovation in action. As we all know, it is usually not enough for a customer to benefit from a great innovation. They want follow-up. They want help in applying the innovation effectively, and they want solutions if it breaks or fails.

Customer service is often the weak link of innovation. One downside to the iPod is it's rather fragile, breaking when stepped on or dropped. After someone stores a lifetime of music preferences on his or her iPod, you can imagine their response when it shatters underfoot. How Apple handles this particular customer-service challenge may well become a very significant factor in the long-term success of the iPod innovation.

The Engines of Innovation

What makes innovation happen? What are the engines of innovation? To me, the most critical engine of innovation, in any organization, is the passionate attitude of people who are liberated to pursue that passion. A truly customer-focused organization will drive innovation because it helps to satisfy the unmet needs of their customers.

It is not uncommon to hear a company claim, *"We are customer focused. Our sales people and our marketing people are deeply engaged with our customers."* This is good – but it's not enough. Sales professionals have a special role with customers. In highly-innovative industries, salespeople are more than a message channel. They act as a special sensing mechanism for the company through a strong, personal relationship with customers. Salespeople are in tune with customer needs which they transmit back to the company. Then, they help galvanize the organization into action.

However, if only sales and marketing people are engaged, innovation will not happen. Innovation happens when *everyone* is passionate and engaged with the customer. Innovation happens when *everyone* plays a part on the team.

Passion for the customer begins at the top – with the CEO. For example, I meet regularly with doctors and other customers in our business. Recently, I met with an expert on infectious disease. He gave me exciting ideas on needed innovations in the treatment of Hepatitis C, an area in which we specialize. I internalized those ideas, and then communicated them to our people working in this area. To me, it's important for people working at Schering-Plough to see this kind of customer engagement from the top.

I stay in close contact with our salespeople and all the other units in the company as well. Our research bench scientists are championing innovative molecules that they believe in – even if commercial data might suggest that there is not a big demand for that molecule. The right attitude is a powerful engine that helps drive innovation.

Another vital engine of innovation is the right behaviors. People are, by instinct, clannish. We tend to be suspicious of other groups, and we like control. But innovation is not achieved by individual genius or by any one unit in a company. The challenge, especially in large, complex organizations, is to break down the natural human and organizational barriers. It means deliberately fostering behaviors that do not come naturally to people or to organizations, such as collaboration, shared accountability and transparency. These behaviors unleash innovation. They unlock the applied creativity of many talents, so that the power of many together is greater than many separately.

It is important to reward the passionate drivers and people who advance innovation through failure.

The passionate drivers do not give up on their cause in the face of the corporate pressures that might otherwise grind them down. These are very important people and they must be nurtured.

Additionally, the people and teams that achieve great failures must also be nurtured. By "great failures," I mean projects that don't become successful innovations, but generate vital information that make future successful innovation possible. How many great failures went into building the iPod?

When I was CEO of a previous company, we acquired a biotech operation. The acquisition itself was something of an innovation. At first, we looked to in-license some of the biotech company's compounds. One morning, while I was shaving, I decided that we should buy the company. Yes, there were risks, but buying the company gave us more than just existing products. We now had a longer-term pipeline. We could bring in the intellectual capital of the biotech's scientists and technologists. We bought the company.

There were big hopes for the lead compound of our newly acquired biotech firm. Guess what? They failed! Two other expensive and energy-consuming projects also failed. People started to lose faith. Investors questioned the acquisition. But, the failures led to progress because a team of passionate drivers in that group did not give up. Six years later, the fourth compound has become a winning innovation. It is now an important, innovative treatment for cancer.

The final engine of innovation is a powerful product flow system. What is this engine? It's a system that channels and maximizes the attitudes and the behaviors I just described with a relentless focus on the customer. In almost every organization that seeks to innovate, there is a front end of research and early creativity. There is a middle that tests, refines and develops the early creativity. Finally, there are the groups that move innovation to the customers: manufacturing, marketing and sales. Supporting these areas are departments such as finance, IT and others.

In conventional organizations, the different units operate as silos. Research is disconnected from development units; R&D is disconnected from marketing and sales. Manufacturing sits in its own silo, and so on. Products move through the pipeline in handoffs over the walls of these silos. Innovation is often lost or compromised. The flow is slow, and response to customer needs is distorted or diluted.

A vital task for any organization is to create seamless interaction between these units, while having them focused and in tune with the customer. Free and easy interaction among the units, combined with strong, transparent operating processes, gating mechanisms, and mutually agreed-upon timeframes make it easier to move products through the system.

An important point of note, in an innovative product flow system, is that progress is not linear. There are loop backs – and loop forwards. However, the progress is not random, but rather purposeful. The looping is creative, productive work that adds value, enhances innovation and makes it more responsive to the needs of the customers.

In my previous company, Pharmacia Corporation, we identified a potentially exciting molecule that could attack infections in a new way. At the time, this was a bold treatment area. Many people still believed that existing antibiotics were all that we needed. Our people had a different vision, one that proved to be correct. Yet, while we had the creativity element in a new family of molecules, we were missing the application and the applied creativity that would transform this discovery into a valuable medicine to doctors and patients. It was a potential innovation, but we were not sure how to get there. We decided to bring the different groups together—research, development, sales & marketing, and manufacturing in a seamless process designed to achieve applied creativity.

Initially, there was a hypothesis that the right approach was to create a treatment that would be effective against a limited number of infections for acute cases. Through conversations with our customers, the teams discovered that doctors had a big need for a powerful new antibiotic that would work against a wide array of infections. The teams looped back and forth, reshaping the focus and refining the compound.

There were further refinements of delivery mechanisms so that treatments could be applied via intravenous drip or in a pill. Clinical trial plans were developed to support regulatory applications for indications that would be most important to the customers. Again, this was accomplished through cross-functional, shared accountability work by research, development, the commercial units and manufacturing. The result was Zyvox – a major innovation in antibiotics. Zyvox was a direct result of customer-focused attitudes, behaviors and systems.

Sustaining Innovation

As the environment keeps changing, organizations must constantly adapt, re-engineer and change how they innovate. There are numerous examples of organizations that failed to sustain innovation. Forty years ago, the U.S. auto industry led the world in innovation.

Detroit was in lock step with its customers. The auto manufacturers kept evolving and changing. Words like *Mustang* and *Thunderbird* conjured up excitement and style.

At a certain point, when the pace of change increased around the world, Detroit fell out of touch. Today, we see U.S. car makers struggling with a very difficult inheritance. They face a downward spiral of performance, a failure in customer focus and the collapse of innovation. In a J.D. Power & Associates survey of buyers, they concluded that a new sedan, the big hope for one U.S. automaker, belonged in the category of "universally disliked." It all comes back to customer focus. Customers and their needs keep evolving. Organizations that seek to innovate must keep evolving with the customers.

Therefore, constantly renewing and re-inventing the organization is the most important duty of the CEO today. Large, global enterprises, ranging from electronics to clothing and fashion; health care to banking need to sustain innovation in order to survive.

At Schering-Plough, we have a model of engaging in constant, transformational change. Our mantra is *New Thinking. New Capabilities. New Urgency.* Our mindset is that this must be led and modeled from the top. And because ours is such a long-term innovation process industry, I will be judged on my performance today for the next 10 to 15 years. The passion to innovate for customers keeps us alive, energized and growing.

CHAPTER 16

Innovation at Avon

By Andrea Jung, chairman and CEO of Avon

Andrea Jung

Andrea Jung gave the Rothman Institute's Fourth Annual CEO Innovation Lecture on November 19, 2009. At the time Jung was chairman and chief executive officer of Avon Products and was responsible for developing and executing all of the company's long-term growth strategies, launching new brand initiatives, developing earnings opportunities for women worldwide, and defining Avon as the premier direct seller of beauty products. Jung was appointed CEO in 1999 and elected chairman in 2001.

Prior to her current role, Jung was president and chief operating officer, with full P&L responsibility for Avon's business units worldwide. From 1996 to 1998, she ascended to senior level positions within Avon's product marketing group, where she oversaw research and development, market research, strategic planning, joint ventures and alliances.

In 2009, Jung was ranked No. 2 on the "FT Top 50 Women in World Business" list by *The Financial Times*; No. 5 on *Fortune* magazine's "50 Most Powerful Women in Business" list; and No. 25 on the *Forbes* list of "The World's 100 Most Powerful Women." In addition, she was ranked one of *The Wall Street Journal's* "50 Women to Watch" and was one of only 18 executives included in *U.S. News & World Report's* "America's Best Leaders 2007."

As of spring 2010, Jung continues leading Avon as it continues its aggressive global expansion.

The role of innovation in business has never been more important than it is right now. The current macro-economic crisis has put tremendous pressure on companies to hunker down as opposed to being bold. However, not every business is bending to the pressures of the economy. Smart companies are moving forward, and they are using innovation to help them navigate the shifting economic landscape. Innovation is their pathway back to prosperity.

The goal for businesses today should be sustainability. Any company can be a one or two year wonder. Unfortunately, success over a longer period of time is not that easy. Long-term success requires innovation. It also demands that a company reinvent itself on an ongoing basis. Innovative leaders stand out by maintaining extraordinary growth on the top line, not just profitability and cost control, allowing them to outperform industry competitors.

One such innovative leader was David McConnell, the founder of Avon. In 1886, Mr. McConnell believed that women should have an opportunity to be economically independent. It was bold and risky, but such moves can often define companies and industries. Our founder believed that women could and should do something outside of the home. It was heresy at the time. In 1886, all direct sales agents were men. Women would not win the right to vote for another 34 years and very few worked outside of the home or earned an independent income. Almost 125 years later, Avon has more than six million independent sales representatives in every corner of the globe who are in effect micro entrepreneurs.

Today, Avon enjoys 90% brand awareness around the world. The company sells four lipsticks every second of the day. We are pioneers in anti-aging skincare and our Anew brand is the number one anti-aging skincare brand globally. We are also number one in fragrance across the developing world. One of the reasons for our success is a $100 million investment to build a world-class research and development facility. Being willing to commit significant capital investment into research and development is critical for developing breakthrough technology in our category, and Avon is a leader in this area.

In addition to our R&D investment, we realized that the company's image needed a makeover as well. Avon would no longer be known as *your grandmother's* brand of lipstick or perfume. We selected Reese Witherspoon as our spokesperson for the Avon brand; Patrick Dempsey is now a face for our men's brand. By combining innovative technology and products that are highly efficacious, but affordable, with powerful imagery, we have modernized Avon's image. We are now routinely listed among the top one hundred global consumer brands in the world.

This transformation of Avon's brand was the first part of the culture of innovation for Avon. The second part focused on the company's distribution channels. When I started at Avon in the mid 1990's, there was great risk in the emerging markets. I was in Russia when the Ruble was devalued. Many of our competitors left the market because of the risk factors but Avon stayed the course. Today, Russia is one of Avon's top three markets. We took the same approach in other emerging markets as well, keeping our eye on the longer term, particularly for the BRIC countries. In 2010, every beauty company wants to do business in Brazil, Russia, India and China. Today, Avon is number one in Latin America as well as in Central and Eastern Europe. We have strong growing businesses in India and China because we were bold enough to be there a decade ago. Other companies are now following suit because the BRIC countries are the major source of domestic demand growth globally in 2010. We project global demand expansion for the next three years will be led by these economies.

Being in the first mover position 15 years ago has yielded significant returns for Avon. In projecting sales for the beauty market through 2013, more than 80% of growth in cosmetics will come from the emerging world markets. We anticipate that Avon will enjoy an out-sized share of growth over the next four years in these markets because of the bet we made a long time ago.

The third part of the culture of innovation at Avon has been the restructuring of the business model for operational excellence. In my first five years as CEO, Avon had consistent double digit top line local currency growth and more than 20% earnings growth. In 2005, my sixth year as CEO, we hit a wall as we faced a new obstacle – competition from global beauty giants such as Unilever and global retailers like Wal-Mart. With pressure to both our brand and channel from these and other global giants, we needed to innovate our operating model so that we could more effectively compete on a global scale against powerful global competitors.

This required one of the most comprehensive transformations in our history. To lead this effort, I had to begin by "innovating" my own personal mindset and also my skills. I had to reinvent myself first before I could reinvent the company.

I remember sitting in my office, late on a Friday night, with my CEO coach. We were discussing different ways to reinvent the company in order to grow our business. He gave me sage advice. "*It all starts with you," he said. "You must go home tonight as if you fired yourself, and come in Monday morning as the new CEO. You will have a new lens to look at your team, your strategies and your organizational structure. But, you will also have access to your past experience and knowledge of the key principles in running Avon. If you can't reinvent your own leadership style, then turning around the company becomes much more difficult.*" His message was clear. The values and the vision and the principles were untouchable; everything else was fair game.

From 2005-08, I wrote the second chapter of my CEO experience at Avon. Whereas formerly the company had been organized into a series of local operating business units, we now added world class global capabilities in marketing, supply chain and sales. Next, we flattened our organization by removing almost a third of the management team. If Avon was going to compete against Wal-Mart and Unilever, we needed to be closer to our customers. The additional layers of management weakened the dialogue with the people buying our products. In addition to this organizational restructuring, we also transformed our cost base, leveraging our global scale in sourcing, and streamlining our product line to focus on global brands. As a result of all these initiatives, we are on our way to freeing up more than $1 billion by 2013. As these benefits have begun to flow over the past several years, we have put a lot of the money back into advertising and marketing to fuel our revenue growth and help us stay competitive.

This restructuring of our operating model set us on a new course of growth between 2005 and 2008. But just as we were ready to claim victory on our new strategic roadmap, we ran smack into the headwinds of one of the worst economic crises in history. Global consumer contraction occurred in every market around the world. We had several meetings where everyone talked about the need to "hunker down" because business was going to be tough. But it quickly became apparent that what was a crisis for the rest of the world could present a tremendous opportunity for Avon, as a company that has historically offered women and families an opportunity to earn an income. I realized that this was a wonderful time to restore excitement and motivation in our company, but that to do so, we would need to once again innovate our thinking and our actions plans to capitalize on this unique opportunity to gain market share even at a time when other companies were retrenching.

Today, Avon looks at job losses around the world and compares those figures to the number of people starting a business with Avon. In every part of our company in any given month, we use recruiting as a metric to motivate our employees. As other companies went through massive layoffs, Avon was offering an earning opportunity to millions of women. When credit markets dried up, people couldn't get loans for their businesses. But Avon in fact is the world's largest micro lender to women. Our sales representatives don't pay us until they get paid by their customers, so on any given day we are extending hundreds of millions of dollars in credit.

To get our message out to the public, when the crisis hit, we launched the most massive recruiting campaign in our company's 124-year history. The marketing and recruiting messages extended from television to the Internet. A year ago, if someone typed *skin care* and *anti-aging* into the Google search bar, Avon would appear on the list. Today, if someone types any phrase indicating they're looking to earn extra money into any search engine, they will see Avon at or near the top of the list. We spend money on search engine optimization knowing that people want solutions to their financial matters. We also launched a major public relations campaign to promote the Avon solution.

Another innovative moment came when Avon advertised on television during the Super Bowl. People scoffed at the idea, telling us, "Budweiser advertises during the Super Bowl, not Avon." Others asked us if we were promoting a new skin care product or lip stick. We said, "Neither. We are going to recruit women to join our growing company by promoting the opportunities available at Avon." Millions of women watch the Super Bowl as well as the pre-game events. In January 2009, our country was entering the heart of the real crisis: real unemployment. It made sense for Avon to promote opportunities with our company.

With these innovations, Avon emerged even stronger from the crisis of 2009. And now in 2010, our focus is on capitalizing on the structural shift that the recession has created on consumer behavior. Consumers have told us in research that spending more than you need to on a product is no longer cool. Now it's cool to be a smart shopper. Looking ahead, the concept of saving money has taken over and transcends all tiers and demographics. If people can find affordable, innovative products, then why spend a lot of money? That's the new consumer mindset in beauty as well as most other categories. I believe this type of consumer is here to stay for awhile. And again, this is our opportunity—to find innovative ways to take advantage of what we're calling the New Normal in consumer behavior.

We are living in interesting times, and I am fortunate to be leading a great company where every employee believes in innovation. Avon is enjoying a transformation because our people were willing to make the necessary changes and reinvent ourselves through innovation. I learned two valuable lessons as the CEO of our company. The first lesson was: *"It's not enough to get new, innovative thoughts into your mind; you need to get the old ones out."* The second lesson I learned, and I will leave you with this thought: *"Let go of assumptions and biases, and keep reinventing yourself. Innovation is the vital spark for all human change, improvement and progress."*

CHAPTER 17

Branding for Success

By Shau-wai Lam, chairman of DCH Auto Group

Shau-wai Lam

Shau-wai Lam gave the Rothman Institute's Twelfth Annual Richard M. Clarke Distinguished Entrepreneurial Lecture on May 5, 2009. At the time Lam was chairman of DCH Auto Group. He joined Dah Chong Hong Trading Corporation (DCH) in 1967. In 1977 DCH began to venture into automobile retailing with its first dealership, Paramus Honda. Lam was later sent to Los Angeles to launch DCH's Western Region in 1979.

After his appointment as president of DCH in 1988, he continued to lead the company's expansion to 25 dealerships in California, New Jersey, New York and Connecticut, with annual sales surpassing $1.83 billion in 2008. Besides winning numerous awards from its franchisors, the DCH Auto Group is proud to have received more of the prestigious J. D. Power and Associates Dealer of Excellence Awards than any dealer group. Lam was the recipient of the 2006 Ellis Island Medal of Honor and the Ernst & Young 2007 New Jersey Entrepreneur of the Year Award for Retail/Distribution Services.

As of spring 2010, Lam continues to lead DCH, overseeing the company's continued growth and maintaining its commitment to giving back to the communities it serves.

Every year, at DCH Auto Group, my colleagues and I assess our company's current position and our potential. Every year, we see a sizeable gap. We are making progress in narrowing the gap, but we still have a long way to go. Our branding strategy for long-term success revolves around closing the gap.

DCH are initials for the Chinese words *Dah Chong Hong*, which means "great prosperous company." That is our vision. DCH (USA) celebrated its 60th anniversary last year, but our history goes back to the 1930s when my father started a trading company in Shanghai. I joined DCH (USA) in 1967 after getting my MBA degree at NYU. At that time, the company had about 15 employees. I was full of enthusiasm and ambition, thinking that I could utilize what I learned at NYU to help grow the company. I was fortunate to have good mentors in my early years with DCH (USA). They taught me how to look at things, and how I should conduct myself. They introduced me to the company's culture, values and heritage that traced back to my father. I still benefit from the teachings, and have incorporated some of the philosophies into my business.

Be willing to let others take advantage of you; in the end you will benefit the most.

This philosophy applies to career advancement as well as customer relations. At work, if you are a dependable performer, you are likely to get more work assigned to you than to your co-workers. Don't complain. By taking on the assignment, you gain more knowledge and experience, improve your efficiency and get to know more people. You may even become the *go-to* person whenever something needs to be done quickly. All these examples increase your value. You end up benefiting more than your co-workers who didn't have to work so hard. If customers know that you are willing to accommodate them, they will prefer to do business with you than with your competitors. You will earn their loyalty and advocacy. It provides you with a future stream of revenue, and it reduces the high marketing cost of acquiring new customers.

Customers are supreme. Serving them takes top priority.

This philosophy came directly from the founding fathers of DCH and has a lot to do with our values and the development of our branding strategy. Employees learned, by heart, a company poem that ended, *Take care of everything for the customer. Bow to thank them for their kind patronage.*

In 1977, with the success of DCH Hong Kong in operating auto dealerships, we decided to enter the U.S. market. Honda was still a relative newcomer in the U.S., but they were expanding their dealer network. We were fortunate to be selected as a new Honda dealer in Paramus, New Jersey. That was our first dealership. More than 30 years later, it is still the flagship store of the DCH Auto Group.

In 2003, we conducted a survey and found that there was very low awareness of the DCH name among consumers. We ran an ad campaign using newspaper, radio and billboards handled by automotive ad agencies. It was costly and there were no measurable results. We didn't move a needle in consumer awareness. We learned the hard way that branding was much more than advertising. We realized we needed help from a branding expert.

In 2005, I hired Larry Light, who had helped McDonald's revive its brand. Larry's company interviewed almost a hundred of our team members at all levels of our dealerships. We then formed a Branding Development Task Force from several layers of management. From our culture and values to customer feedback on experience and expectations, we identified our brand essence. We drafted a Brand Promise, defined its key elements and developed our Plan to Win. We had a final meeting with top management and brought them up to speed.

What is a brand?

A brand reflects the purpose of the company, its spirit and its values. A brand is developed collaboratively within the company. A great brand gives team members a feeling of purpose and pride. A brand is a promise to team members that, if you work for this brand, you will get a positive experience. It's also a promise to consumers that if they buy the brand, then they will get a positive experience as well.

For customers of DCH, they receive our Brand Promise which makes them feel *welcome, respected, productive, confident* and *enthused.* Each of these five words defines the desired DCH experience for every customer, every day, at every DCH dealership. Together they are the DCH Way.

After deciding on our Brand Promise, we went on to develop our Plan to Win. In the plan, we identified the six P's that would affect our ability to deliver our Brand Promise: *people, product, place, price, promotion* and *performance.* In the section "Where We Want to Be," we listed our mission statement, the five key elements of the DCH Way and our Brand Promise of delivering a comforting experience. In "How We Plan to Get There," we listed the work requirements for each of the P's. For "How We Measure Progress," we included performance measurement factors to track our progress. Finally, we assessed our ability to carry out the functions in each of the P's. We were ready to start the process of our internal launch in the spring of 2007.

Kick-off events and sessions were held on each coast for all managerial employees. We created a new position of Corporate Brand Experience Manager to develop enterprise-wide guidelines for marketing and advertising. Each dealership was allowed to customize its own message while reinforcing the brand image. Next, we conducted mini-launch events at each dealership location to bring the message to every team member. The dealership general manager and department managers also participated in the presentations to demonstrate their support and commitment. The next steps were the preparation of the external launch and promotion — that is, raising public awareness of the DCH Auto Group Brand and building trust in the minds of consumers.

In the external brand marketing phase, we implemented "cause branding" programs that required only a small budget, but that would have a widespread impact. These programs got our dealers personally involved in a worthy cause in the community, and brought positive media attention and favorable comments. Our employees felt proud to be members of the DCH Auto Group.

In 2008, we selected Teen Safe Driving as our cause branding campaign. According to the Insurance Institute for Highway Safety, car accidents are the main cause of teenage fatalities. In 2006, more than 5,000 teens died and 300,000 were injured in auto related accidents. We believed that most of the accidents were preventable if teens followed precautionary measures. Given our role in selling and servicing automobiles, we knew we could help. It was a natural fit for our company.

We sought an alliance with a reputable, nonprofit organization that advocated safe teen driving. We selected SADD – Students Against Destructive Decisions. SADD helps high schools nationwide set up and maintain SADD chapters at their schools. Teens listen to each other, and sometimes they are more effective in educating and influencing their peers; SADD chapters provide teams with a forum to help achieve their objectives.

DCH became the exclusive automobile dealership sponsor of SADD in all of New Jersey; southern New York state; southern Connecticut and southern California. DCH employees now work with students from local schools to launch SADD chapters by providing both financial and personal support. Throughout the school year, our dealerships sponsor events and support teen efforts to educate their peers on the importance of good driving behavior.

We also engaged a very creative ad agency, The Joey Company, to help design and develop a theme for our teen safe driving campaign, and to prepare for phase two of our advertising campaign. With their help, we created a long-term community outreach program called *Mindless Driving. Keep It Out of Cars.* Materials were designed and printed. Each dealership received at least one kiosk featuring the campaign and our partnership with SADD.

In October, we held events on both coasts with senior officers of SADD and students from SADD chapters. In November, DCH Freehold Nissan staged a safety fair. Four radio stations promoted the free event and local businesses donated all the food. The entire fair cost the dealership almost nothing and it generated a lot of good publicity. Our dealership teams continue to build relationships with more high schools and community leaders. Additionally, more SADD chapters are being launched.

Currently, we are preparing to launch phase two. With the help of The Joey Company, we will expand our *Mindless Driving. Keep It Out of Cars* program. Our advertising campaign is ready to go, and we will utilize third-party endorsements to help build consumer trust. At the same time, we want to improve the effectiveness of our grassroots and Internet marketing.

Some people ask us, "With the auto industry undergoing a severe downturn, is this the right time to move forward with our branding strategy?" Our answer is we must keep the momentum going. We can't pull back. We must keep making deposits in our branding bank.

CHAPTER 18

Creating a Business from Scratch

*By Diahann Lassus, co-founder
and president of Lassus Wherley*

Diahann Lassus

Diahann Lassus gave the Rothman Institute's Inaugural Female Entrepreneur Lecture on March 26, 2004. At the time she was co-founder and president of Lassus Wherley & Associates, P.C., a wealth management firm with offices in New Jersey and Florida.

Lassus was named one of *Worth Magazine's* "Top Financial Advisors" for an unprecedented five times. Her expertise has been recognized at all levels of government. President Bill Clinton appointed Lassus to the Retirement Savings Summit in Washington, D.C. She was also a delegate to the White House Conference on Small Business, for which she chaired the New Jersey Capital Formation Committee.

For more than 30 years, Lassus has been focused on finance — holding positions at Blue Cross-Blue Shield, Western Electric, and AT&T in areas that include assessment and analysis, as well as serving as AT&T's field operations manager for its Special Project Olympic Operations in Los Angeles.

As of spring 2010, Lassus continues to grow Lassus Wherley and gain national recognition for herself and the firm.

In 1983, I was recruited for the core team to help build the 1984 summer Olympics in Los Angeles. It was probably the most incredible experience I ever had in my life. I was responsible for the field operations teams, including: the computer systems out in the field, the telephone systems for the volunteers and the technical people to help the athletes. We had 700 people working in three shifts around the clock at the different Olympic sites all over Southern California.

I was 31 years old at the time and working at an Executive VP level with 13 levels of people reporting to me. In a normal environment, I'm sure the roles would be reversed, and I would be reporting to them. When it was over, I ended up in Atlanta at another job. I was in charge of consolidating the accounts payable for three regions. It was a completely different challenge. After working 20 hours a day, seven days a week, for nine months, my new job seemed much more reasonable. In other words, it was boring.

I was offered early retirement at the age of 32. Thinking that I probably had some good years left in me, I went looking for the next challenge. I decided to start my own company. My business partner was my boss and mentor on the L.A. Olympic project. We decided to start a consulting firm. We both knew about customer service, warehousing, and marketing. As the business plan came together, we realized that we had strengths in other areas as well, namely dealing with people and financial issues. Coincidentally, we stumbled across the Certified Financial Planner® designation in *Money* magazine. I signed up and wrote my first financial plan halfway through the first course.

A key part of our business model was to create something that previously hadn't existed. We wanted to bring different professional services together under one roof--Certified Financial Planners®, CPAs, attorneys and investment people. Unfortunately, we were ahead of the curve and there were numerous rules and regulations that slowed us down. The early development was tough. We were good at managing and documenting. We understood the importance of teams and many things about business. We knew how to target market and get a product to market. But, there was one area that we didn't know anything about—we didn't know how to sell. It was a real eye-opener for us.

We sold financial planning services back when no one knew about financial planning services. We called it Comprehensive Financial Planning. The business looked at both personal and business cash flow statements and financial objectives. We asked our clients, *"Where are you now? Where do you want to be tomorrow? How do you plan to get there?"* We took basic logic from business courses and applied it to the financial planning process. It was very successful...when we got someone in the door. They liked what we were doing. Our objective was to figure out how to get more clients in the door.

Part of our success was based on the fact that *we* believed when nobody else believed in us. We were structured in a corporate way when most small firms were focused with getting customers in the door. We were structured as a team; we had teams when there were only three of us. It's about understanding what it is you want to accomplish and finding different ways of doing it.

To be successful as an entrepreneur, you must learn how to stand out, and not blend in. If you go to a class or meeting and you want to be noticed, you sit in the front of the room. You also wear bright colors, raise your hand and ask questions. You do these things to be remembered. That is exactly what we did. We wore red suits, sat in the front row, stood up to ask questions, addressed the entire group and said our name before we spoke.

Another area that has contributed to our success is a high rate of retention. Relationships are key. It's not enough to win the business; you need to hold onto it. The same principle is true with employees. We hire part-time people and see them as an important asset to our company. The young man who runs our data information systems is currently a sophomore at college. He just celebrated his five-year anniversary with us. We hire high school students and they stay with us. We train them so well that other companies want to hire them away from us.

We always have a different view of the world than our competitors because we have so many young people in our firm. And they get involved. Everyone in the company is on one of two teams. The person's job doesn't matter; they have to be on a team. The teams have objectives and they develop strategies. It's incredibly energizing. The focus of the teams is twofold: How do we stay ahead of the competition and how do we retain our clients?

The last area that has contributed to our success comes from our belief that the power of many is stronger than the power of one. When we realized that we couldn't get the necessary services from existing trust companies, we put together our own trust company with 100 other firms around the country. Now, we are offering lower-cost services because we don't have to do marketing. We have 108 offices around the country with shareholders who utilize the trust company. When we leverage the $40 billion controlled by the shareholders, we have more clout. We also have access to a number of top experts in our industry. It's like having a personal think tank. We meet twice a year and share ideas. The trust company controls $1.6 billion after less than three years in existence.

If you are looking for a takeaway from this talk, remind yourself to never get too comfortable with your business model—no matter how effective it might be today. Set up a system of checks and balances to confirm that (1) what you are doing, (2) how you are doing it, and (3) your customers and potential customers are all in alignment with your goals and objectives. Be the driver of your business.

CHAPTER 19

Social Entrepreneurship: Doing Good While Doing Well

by Lillian Rodríguez López,
president of the Hispanic Federation

Lillian Rodríguez López

Lillian Rodríguez López gave the Rothman Institute's Fifth Annual Female Entrepreneur Lecture on March 28, 2008. At the time she was president of the Hispanic Federation, a nonprofit membership organization serving more than 90 Latino health and human service agencies in New York, New Jersey, Connecticut and Pennsylvania. Rodríguez López first joined the Federation in 1996 as vice president. Under her leadership, the Federation has dramatically increased its organizational capacity to serve an ever-increasing network of member agencies and respond to the Latino community's needs locally and nationally.

Prior to joining the Hispanic Federation, Rodríguez López was employed at the New York City Health and Hospitals Corporation (HHC), a public benefit corporation which oversees the city's health-care system, in several capacities including executive assistant to the chairman of the board of directors. She serves as a member of Citizens Union, the Wachovia Bank Community Board and the Manhattan Borough President Community Board Reform Committee.

As of spring 2010, Rodríguez López continues to lead the Federation.

Running a non-profit is a lot like running a business. Your contributions are your revenues, your funders are your clients, and your business is health and human services. But, we manage businesses with a heart. Our imperative is the social good of the communities and the people we serve. My drivers are the betterment of Latino institutions and the Latino community. The areas we focus on for progress include: education, health, arts and culture, and housing and small business development, to name a few. Like a business, we need to manage our resources effectively, namely people and money. We analyze trends, have clear decision-making parameters and change course when necessary.

There are four rules I learned while running a non-profit business that translate well for running any kind of business. First, if you give yourself the *no*, no one else will have to. Second, if it was easy, everyone would be doing it. Third, if you stand for nothing, you will fall for everything. And finally, you can do good and do well at the same time.

One example of my first rule happened when I was 18 years old. I was asked to manage a summer youth employment program in the Bronx. It was my first big job. I was responsible for the summer work placement and payroll of 300 youths, some older than me. I was from the Bronx but would be traveling to places that, in the early 80's, were considered tough neighborhoods. I still said yes to the job, not because I was confident, but because I was stupid. I didn't know what I was getting myself into, but figured as long as I had the energy and commitment to figure things out, I could do the job. It wasn't the easiest summer I ever had, but I prevailed. To this date, I am grateful for the experience of my first job. It helped prepare me for the pressures and other difficult work environments of future jobs. I learned that, if I gave myself challenging experiences, I could call on the reserves of character that were built in earlier times. If I didn't take that job, I might not be in my position today.

Be unrealistic and take risks. Let other people – your mother, your father and grandmother – be cautious for you. Raise the expectations that you have for yourself and you will be your strongest ally. Remember to collect the different experiences that you will need in the world of entrepreneurship. The negative experiences are part of your life, so don't regret the things you do – regret the things that you don't do. All experiences teach us something about ourselves and our world.

The second rule is *"If it was easy, everybody would be doing it."* Do you see thousands of people accomplishing what the female CEOs of PepsiCo, Avon, or BET have accomplished? No, because it takes discipline, perseverance and dedication in order to achieve that level of success. It means late nights without TiVo, reading reports and policy papers and being nice to people that you don't like – that you *really* don't like! It means sacrificing short-term personal wants for long-term, hard-to-accomplish career goals. Very few people are capable of taking on this challenge.

Creating a business or getting ahead is not for the faint-of-heart. If you want to grow in your role, you have to step out of your comfort zone. When I came to the Hispanic Federation in 1996, I was given progressively more responsibility. In 1998, the president decided to move on and I was appointed president during the interim period. For several months, I was acting president, and I thought these people were nuts for letting me run the place. The President's role requires certain competencies – in fundraising, media savvy, public policy analysis and financial management. In assuming the job, I realized that, in my two years at the Hispanic Federation, I learned enough in the critical areas of the business to manage the organization.

In 2004, six years later, I became President of the Federation.

My former boss, whom I succeeded, is now the Secretary of State for New York. Lorraine Cortes-Vazquez became the first Hispanic to serve in this position in New York. I adore her and greatly respect her, but sometimes hated her when we worked together. Why? She always pushed me to do more – public speaking, panel presentations, awards, budgets and contracting. If I told her I didn't want to do something, I then had to do it! If she believed that a job or project was critical to my leadership or managerial development – I had to do more of it! We always said to each other, "This is not easy." Well, the important things in life aren't always supposed to be easy. Sometimes we get tested. There is a saying, *"If you want something bad enough, you will find a way; if you don't, you will find an excuse."* Do you want to get the job done, or do you want to go watch television?

My third rule is, *"If you stand for nothing, you will fall for everything."* I am in the business of health and human services, developing communities and institutions and working to better lives. Many things affect my ability to do my job: public policy, legislation, government budgets, as well as other interests related to politics, race, business and more. When the comprehensive immigration reform bill was introduced into Congress last year, it was hotly debated. The bill, which would determine the fate of over 12 million undocumented immigrants in this country, had many complicated and intricate provisions. The Federation joined with other national organizations to analyze and understand the bill's impact on a vulnerable immigrant community. The central questions were: Are undocumented workers a threat to the economy, lawfulness and security of this country? Or, do they reflect the history and true fiber of this country and deserve an opportunity to openly and legally work and prosper here? What stood in the balance was huge for the undocumented immigrants - American citizenship that would lead to many benefits and opportunities.

The Federation opposed the bill and it did not get through the Senate. People have asked us how we could oppose the bill. Wouldn't it have created opportunities for these individuals and families? The answer was no. The bill would have locked us, potentially for decades, into a system that did not value family reunification, that would send individuals and even their families back to their home countries to apply for citizenship, and that would have created a guest worker program that sent workers back home every two years for an entire year. It was, in our estimation, overwhelmingly punitive and financially burdensome. We stood for what we thought was just and fair and believed that the bill went against true American values.

As business leaders and entrepreneurs, you need to know what you stand for — determine your values as they relate to workers, diversity, negotiations, competition, and wealth accumulation. The challenge is to know when to bend, but not to break, and when to stand firmly for the values you hold dear.

This brings me to my final thoughts about doing good and doing well. Regardless of where you find yourself in life, you can give back in the forms of time, money and obligations. Why obligations? Because we have to acknowledge that we stand on the shoulders of others — that we must look back and bring others along in the way we have been guided and supported in our lives. If you are doing well in terms of your personal wealth, influence and power, imagine how much good you can do if you choose to share those things and unleash them. Choose to make yourself a powerful statement of progress and do good.

CHAPTER 20

Justice and Social Entrepreneurship

By Ralph Nader, consumer advocate

Ralph Nader

Ralph Nader spoke at the Institute's Social Entrepreneurship Conference on September 16, 2009. He is a consumer advocate and former presidential candidate who has devoted his life to giving ordinary people the tools they need to defend themselves against corporate negligence and government indifference. He has been honored as "One of the 100 Most Influential Figures in American History" by *The Atlantic Magazine*.

Nader, one of today's foremost social entrepreneurs, has organized millions of citizens into hundreds of citizen groups that he helped start. They include the Center for Auto Safety, Public Citizen, Pension Rights Center, Disability Rights Center, and student Public Interest Research Groups.

Working with lawmakers, Nader was instrumental in creating the Occupational Safety and Health Administration, the Environmental Protection Agency, and the Consumer Product Safety Commission. Laws he helped draft and pass include the Safe Drinking Water Act, meat and poultry inspection rules, air pollution control laws, the Freedom of Information Act and hundreds of others. His efforts have saved hundreds of thousands of lives and made healthier many millions more.

As of spring 2010, he continues to be the most influential consumer advocate in the United States.

I have been asked to talk about myself a little bit — which I do not like to do — because people want to know how I built organizations like Public Citizen and Single Payer Action. So I'll spend a few minutes, with your indulgence, on how I came to this kind of work. Now, what is this kind of work? It is not charity, it's justice. There is a significant difference between charity and justice. Charity, to take one example, is administering to hungry people in a soup kitchen, which is very important. Justice is asking, "What are the causes of hunger in America, the richest country in the world?"

Justice is the greatest engine of economic growth and, above all, redistributed economic growth. It means that people who work hard get their just desserts — which millions of American workers are not getting these days. It's integral to the development of a society dedicated to fulfilling life's possibilities of the greatest number of people in its midst. That's why, in talking about social responsibility of corporations and social entrepreneurship, the real propulsion comes from people who stand up against an injustice, who alert people of far greater number to it and then mobilize injustice movements. The social entrepreneurship part comes in finding ways to build and support these movements through reallocating resources. That way justice organizations can thrive and become true agents of change and economic growth.

In the 1950's, I went to Princeton, not far from here, and I was appalled one day when they were spraying DDT on all the trees on that beautiful campus. Then early in the morning I would come back to my dorm from studying and I would see all these dead birds on the sidewalk. And they weren't mutilated. They were just dead as if something got to them. So I picked up a couple of them and took them down to the daily Princetonian paper and I said, "There's something wrong here." I was a sophomore, and the senior with his legs on the desk — watch out when you go to a reporter and his legs are on the desk; there's a certain complacency there — he said, "I don't think anything's wrong. We have the smartest biology and chemistry professors around, and if there is a connection between the two, they certainly would have sounded the alarm." And that's when I learned one of my greatest lessons: that it doesn't matter how much you know if you don't have fire in your belly.

Later, I went to Harvard Law School, and I used to hitchhike a lot. I'd be picked up by truck drivers, and occasionally we would be first at the scene of a crash, before the police and the ambulances. It left an indelible impact on me. When you talk about violence and mayhem, try looking at what happens to people in a crash: in a two-car collision, truck collision, or a crash against an abutment. The screams, the cries, the ominous silence. You just can't forget that.

I went back to the law school and I decided to write a paper on engineering stagnation and legal liability. The auto companies in Detroit couldn't produce the most obvious safety features that had been in use and patented for years: seatbelts, head restraints, padded dash panels, collapsing steering columns that won't spear you in a left-front collision and stronger door latches so you're not spilled out — nothing that required any Einsteinian genius.

So I would write the auto companies and say, "I'm a law student at Harvard. I'd like some information about the safety of your cars." And they would send back their latest brochures about their latest model-year cars, which didn't mention safety. Safety was a taboo. Safety was a downer. So I wondered, "How could anybody be so successful in business and be so stupidly lethal, so indifferent, and so callous?" Their own families drove in those cars. And in the pursuit of that, I wrote a third-year paper and turned it into a book, *Unsafe at Any Speed*. There was a big congressional hearing in the spring of 1966, a few months after the book came out in November 1965. In a very rapid fashion, this giant industry came under federal regulation, with two motor vehicle and highway safety laws that Lyndon Johnson signed in September 1966. You see how fast Congress acted in those days?

After we got this law through, I became very famous and got a lot of lecture invitations. I could go to any conference, even Davos in Switzerland. But I said to myself, "I don't want to be a lone ranger." I wanted to proliferate the number of citizen advocacy groups. I wanted to bring in thousands of students from colleges, high schools, business schools and law schools. The *Washington Post* called them Nader's Raiders, and that was a nice moniker. We started investigating various governmental agencies — the Department of Agriculture, Food and Drug Administration, Interstate Commerce Commission — and then we had a major investigation of Congress where we put out 35-page profiles on every member of Congress, to their endless consternation, and distributed it back home.

My job was to be a Johnny Appleseed. It was to give a lot of opportunities to people to work as full-time citizens, to get them to work all over the country, to get them to work in all sectors of the political economy, and to recognize that when you change social values to a level of higher priority you create economic internalization of those values, which creates jobs. So we increased the public awareness of safety in motor vehicles — crash-worthy safety, better brakes, better tires, etc. — and what happened? Well, there are thousands of workers today who are producing airbags and seatbelts. The environmental laws created markets for companies to produce fire detection equipment, safety devices and pollution control systems for coal plants, etc. So there is this natural flow between the nonprofit advocacy world and the development of entrepreneurs or established companies who wake up to their social responsibilities.

Let me suggest, very briefly, some ways to build democratic institutions.

Decades after I graduated, I went back to Princeton and I said to a few of my classmates, "Let's organize our class so that we provide citizen advocacy opportunities for students. When they're on summer break, we'll place them in citizen groups around the country." We started Princeton Project 55 and we placed more people directly and indirectly than the Princeton placement office. It is now an established tradition at Princeton, and we are inspiring other universities' alumni to form their own groups. It occurred to me at the time: Look at that incredible affinity group — the alumni class, thousands of alumni classes moving into the 30th and 35th year, knowing each other since they were 17 and 18. Look at the enormous civic power that can come out of that because these classes have almost every talent. They have business talent, legal talent, engineering talent, medical talent, accounting talent, graphics art talent, and computer talent. And so that's one whole new source of gestating democratic institutions.

The second source that's often not viewed — remember when we got refunds? When the California Public Utilities Commission catches Pacific Gas & Electric overcharging its customers, they require hundreds of millions of dollars to be refunded. Well, there should be a check-off on the refund so if you don't want your $15 or $30 refund, you can assign it to a nonprofit consumer group that monitors the California utility industry so they can have their own economists, their own lawyers, their own organizers and their own educators tipping the balance of power a little bit more in the favor of the consumer-payers. It was never thought of by the regulatory agencies, but it's a possibility. A lot of time when you have class actions and you have hundreds of millions of dollars to distribute to the aggrieved consumers, they can't find a lot of the consumers to send them back what they were cheated. So there should be trust funds to create institutions to prevent the very kind of fraud, price fixing or deceptive practice that the class action had exposed. That's another whole area of civic activity.

The third one is to elaborate on the student public interest research groups. And at many universities now, due to our efforts like New Hampshire Public Interest Research Group and New Jersey PIRG and so on, students can check off $5, $6, or $7 to be added to their tuition bill, which goes into a nonprofit group run by elected students. They hire the young scientists, lobbyists or lawyers to advance justice in their state. New Jersey PIRG did terrific work analyzing violations of water permit regulations by polluters in the streams and rivers of New Jersey. Then there's the simple concept of the check-off itself. Every time we get a bill from an insurance company or a bank statement — and it can be done electronically too — we could be given the opportunity to basically check off a certain amount of money that goes into an oversight group.

Now if we had these oversight groups, we wouldn't have as much hospital-induced infections, because patients will have been organized through these check-offs into a nonprofit consumer oversight group. We would have had the bank depositors catch a lot of the shenanigans with the banks on the corner of Main and Elm or on Wall Street much earlier. Whenever you want to improve a society, let the beneficiaries of the society's economy or the victims organize themselves — whether they're workers, taxpayers, consumers, shareholders, or investors. What we are seeing in this country is a huge mismatch between the organized power of vendors and the organized power of government compared to the unorganized nature of voters, taxpayers, workers, consumers, and other roles that we play as recipients of public and private decision-making.

I'll leave you with a little aphorism from ancient China. Here it is: To know and not to do is not to know. We know how to deal with 25,000 children who die every day from the most easily prevented causes like contaminated water. We know how to deal with a more benign environment and how to protect our soil, land, and water. We are way, way, way ahead of our knowledge compared to our implementation. Our priorities are so out of kilter that they can be defined as institutional insanity. The World Health Organization budget is the equivalent of the budget of the Peter Brent Brigham Hospital. It's smaller than Columbia Presbyterian. The U.N. budget is smaller than the budget of Harvard University.

We have to tell ourselves, if we want to get something done, we have to put the resources in. If someone wants to build a steel mill, they don't start with $300,000, do they? They put the resources in. We have to do the same in the civic arena.

CHAPTER 21

Buying and Selling Entrepreneurial Companies

By Gregory Olsen, president of GHO Ventures,
and co-founder of Sensors Unlimited

Gregory Olsen

Dr. Gregory Olsen, BS '66, BSEE '68, MS '68, gave the Rothman Institute's Eighth Annual Richard M. Clarke Distinguished Entrepreneurial Lecture on May 3, 2006. At the time Olsen had recently become the third private citizen to orbit the Earth on the International Space Station.

After an illustrious career as a research scientist and entrepreneur, Olsen, president of GHO Ventures, manages his "angel" investments and speaks to student audiences — especially minorities and women — encouraging them to consider careers in science and engineering.

Olsen co-founded EPITAXX, a fiber-optic detector manufacturer in 1984, and sold it in 1990. In 1991, he co-founded Sensors Unlimited, a near-infrared camera manufacturer and sold it in 2000.

As of spring 2010, Olsen continues his work as a leading angel investor in the region and as a lecturer who inspires young and old alike to focus on their education and pursue their dreams.

After obtaining my degree from FDU, I spent the next 11 years working as a standard research scientist at RCA labs. One day at work, the entrepreneurial bug bit me. I wanted to start a business. In 1983, with no formal training and no business background, a partner and I took a small amount of venture capital money and started a fiber optics business.

We had all the usual start-up problems, including running short on money and struggling with payroll. However, after five years, we managed to build up a pretty profitable business. In 1990, my company was acquired by Nippon Sheet Glass. After we were acquired, I stayed on for a year, then drifted off and started another business; a typical entrepreneurial move.

It might be worth noting that my company, EPITAXX, was acquired by JDS Uniphase during the fiber optics boom. They eventually employed over a thousand people. I think employing that many people is as satisfying as any financial numbers one might achieve. After EPITAXX, I started a company called Sensors Unlimited. My business partner was Marshall Cohen. He knew a lot about sensing; I knew how to make the chips. It was a good marriage.

One of the best early moves we made was tapping into the Small Business Innovation Research program. The SBIR is a government funded program which provides up to $750,000 for small businesses with very few strings attached. It's a great system of venture capital that you don't have to pay back. We used money from the SBIR program plus our own money to get the company off the ground.

By 1998, telecom was picking up dramatically, and it was feeding the Internet. By 2000, we were doubling our sales every year and things were red hot. Those were the days when everyone knew stock was worth more than cash. Sensors Unlimited was acquired by Finistar

Corporation in 2000 for $600 million. In retrospect, it was a huge number, but that's what happened in those days.

Eighteen months after our acquisition, the stock market crashed. In 2000, when we were acquired by Finistar, their stock was trading at $35. In 2002, it had fallen to 50 cents. We bought our company back from Finistar, in a management buyout, for $6 million. We knew the company had good people and good technology. The problem was with the overall market. Telecom and fiber optics spending plummeted.

We struggled for the next 18 months and had over $1 million in losses. During that period, we reinvented ourselves. Sensors Unlimited went from being a fiber optics producer into infrared sensing. After a year and a half, we got to break even, and then profitable. We did it the old fashioned way with hard work and watching the pennies. In 2005, we were acquired by Goodrich Corporation for $60 million.

From starting two companies and having one that I sold, bought back and sold again, I gained valuable knowledge about starting, running and selling companies. I learned that the best time to sell a company is when prices are going up! I remember going to a technical conference on fiber optics in 2000. It was like going to a rock concert; people were lined up out the door. I watched the value of our company go up by a factor of ten in less than a year. That is a good time to sell.

The second thing I learned is to buy your company back when the market has bottomed out! In just two short years, the stock market crashed. At that point, stocks were worthless, and cash was king. The technical conferences were almost empty. Sensors Unlimited, like most acquisitions, became a cash burden to their parent company. I saw valuations drop by a factor of 10. It was a good time to buy, and that's what we did.

In the period from repurchasing the company to when we sold

ourselves again, Sensors Unlimited underwent a reinvention with a slight twist. We switched from fiber optics to infrared imaging, but we did it all with the same people, the same building and the same basic technology. In 2005, we had about $17 million in sales and $3 million in profit. Those were realistic numbers for a sale price.

People asked us, "If you had such good financial numbers, why did you sell?" The main reason is something that often happens when selling in markets like the military or the pharmaceutical industry; you need to team up with a strong partner. For example, if the government buys something from a small company, even if it's the best product at the best price, they want to have the confidence that you will be around in three years when they need replacements, repairs, etc. Therefore, it helps to be associated with names such as Boeing or Raytheon. In our case, we were in the aerospace military market. We needed a solid partner.

In looking back at my entrepreneurial endeavors, I find that it helps to understand how different indicators affect a company's ability to operate in the marketplace. For example, in 1984 when I started my first business, it was very difficult to raise capital, but it was easy to hire people. Unemployment was high and companies had been closing down. There was a lot of empty space so we could cut good deals with landlords.

In 1990, it was easy to get money, but all the good people were employed. It was tough finding qualified people and rents were at an all time high during that period. We needed leverage, or something we could trade. In 1992, when we started Sensors Unlimited, we didn't have a lot of money. We were basically a semi conductor business and we needed equipment that cost millions of dollars, but we didn't have that kind of money.

However, we did have research contracts. We also had a partnership with Princeton University which had equipment, but didn't have the research support. We used our leverage by sharing research contracts as well as people. We had our engineers help Princeton University run their lab. In return, we got to use their laboratory space. We successfully used our leverage.

We had a good working environment at Sensors Unlimited because we did things the old fashioned way. We didn't do flex time. We focused on the business, which started at 8:00 AM and went until 5:00 PM. It was all business too. I've found that, if you run a business in a professional manner, you get professional results.

If you run a good company that has a solid work environment, then your employees become your best recruiters. We had those employees in place and we developed our own culture. One thing about successful businesses is that they all have some sort of culture. Another thing that helped us was forming lots of partnerships. It was difficult working in a vacuum.

Our offices were about three miles from Princeton University. I had a good relationship with Steve Forrest, a Professor of Electrical Engineering there. I worked with Steve before he started teaching at Princeton. In fact, he started at the University about the same time I started my company, so it was a nice synergy and we helped each other out. We also did work with Sarnoff Corporation, Rutgers, NJIT, and all the New Jersey universities.

Another piece of advice is if you have a business in New Jersey or within the area, I strongly recommend joining the New Jersey Technology Council. It is one of the best networking organizations for entrepreneurial companies. I have gotten so much out of working with them. To me, it's a no-brainer for people looking to start a business or ones that are already in business.

One of the most satisfying parts of building two businesses is that, even though we drew millions of dollars from the government in terms of research programs, we produced some great technology. When we sold our companies, we were able to pay back both the state and the federal government in the form of tax money. The system does work if you play it correctly. If you're smart about the way you use government money, their payback should come at tax time.

8 More Things I Learned From Starting and Selling Two Businesses:

1. Lean and mean is better.
2. Hire people who are smarter than you.
3. Once you've hired those people, let them do their jobs. Don't micro-manage them.
4. Mistakes are a part of every business. It doesn't matter if it's your first business or your fifth business. Your goal should be to cut the time between when a mistake is made and when it's fixed.
5. Cash is king.
6. Buy low and sell high.
7. Profits trump growth.
8. Fewer people in a group will work harder and make it better.

In the end, business is not really about technology and/or the markets. Fundamentally, it's about people. If you have the right people in your business, the probability of success is high. Remember these three things: Be persistent, survive your mistakes, and focus on the people.

CHAPTER 22

The Story Behind SwitchFlops

by Lindsay Phillips, founder, SwitchFlops, Inc.

Lindsay Phillips

Lindsay Phillips gave the Rothman Institute's Seventh Annual Female Entrepreneur Lecture on March 26, 2010. At the time, she was the energetic inspiration and founding force behind her namesake company and the now-famous SwitchFlops. Her footwear concept evolved from a high school art project—ceramic flip flops. Amazed by the response, Lindsay began designing functional flops with colorful straps, each adorned by a unique button. Her idea evolved when she realized that by using hook-and-loop fasteners she could create one shoe with many straps–unlimited choices with minimal effort. This simple, yet brilliant innovation was the birth of SwitchFlops. Lindsay applied for a patent on her idea before she graduated high school.

During her college years Lindsay perfected her interchangeable design. Her travels to Europe for classes and her voyage around the world on the Semester at Sea exposed her to a kaleidoscope of cultures, colors, and patterns that would influence her strap designs. Lindsay honed her design, merchandising and manufacturing skills working summers at Polo Ralph Lauren's leather goods division in New York City. After her patent was granted in 2004, she joined forces with her mother, Liz, to start her business and find a manufacturer. SwitchFlops made its retail debut in January 2007 at the Surf Expo Trade Show in Orlando where it was showcased as a new and innovative product. Orders started rolling in and explosive growth followed.

Thomas Edison once said, *"Genius is one percent inspiration and ninety-nine percent perspiration."* As a fellow inventor — based upon my experiences in coming up with an idea, getting it patented, finding an overseas manufacturer and going to market with the final product — I would have to agree.

When I was in high school, I designed a pair of ceramic sandals for an art project. They were OK, but I thought I could make them even cooler by adorning them with a bunch of funky buttons. My art teacher loved the sandals and submitted them to a competition. Unfortunately, they didn't win because they weren't a "pure ceramic piece."

I was disappointed about the competition, but decided that I wanted to make a real pair of sandals. I purchased a pair of inexpensive flip-flops, some funky buttons and glue. When I glued the buttons to the flip-flops, they wouldn't stay put. I needed to figure out a way to keep the buttons from falling off.

The answer was Velcro. It was an *a-ha* moment! I bought some Velcro and started lining the shoes with it. I made the tops and stitched on the buttons. The buttons stayed put. I made samples for my family and everyone loved them. A family friend who saw the flip-flops suggested I get a patent so that no one could steal my idea.

When I went to a local patent attorney, he said *"I don't want to discourage you, but just because it's not already on the market doesn't mean that someone doesn't have a patent for it."* He suggested I save the thousand dollars it would cost me to hire him by doing some homework on the Internet first. He gave me a Web site to see if I could find any examples of people using my idea.

Every day after school, I got on the computer and searched for anything that looked remotely like what I was doing. After a week of not finding any examples, I went back to the attorney. He agreed to help me apply for the patent. Surprisingly, it took four years to actually get the patent. By this time, I was a sophomore in college. However, with a patent in hand, my mother and I decided to launch our company. We were going to make SwitchFlops!

The first thing I had to do was find a manufacturer. My mother was a nurse and my father was a doctor. They had no manufacturing experience. I went online and found names of local manufacturers. I also contacted people in the flip-flop industry. Unfortunately, I couldn't manufacture my product in the U.S. because I was too much of a risk and my minimum order was too low. If I was going to make this happen, I had to go overseas. With my parents' help, I started networking to find someone to help me make an overseas connection. Eventually, a family friend introduced us to someone with connections to factories and translators in China.

My mother and I flew to China and went to our first factory. It was quite an experience. I showed the factory owner my homemade prototype. He liked it and agreed to work with us. We placed an order for 5,000 shoes and 4,500 straps. Because it was a brand-new concept, it took us two years of tweaking to get a working prototype.

In December 2006 our first order of 5,000 SwitchFlops and 4,500 straps arrived at my parents' house. If I didn't want to personally own these shoes for the rest of my life, I needed to learn how to sell them. Once again, I got on the Internet, did my research and then went to a few local retailers. I asked them how they found different products for their stores. Almost all of them told me to exhibit my SwitchFlops at trade shows.

It was back to the Internet for more research. This time I was looking for local trade shows. I found one called the Surf Expo. Coincidentally, they had a program for new companies that provided free booth space for up to five promising startups at each show. I applied and won a booth at the show.

In January 2007 I started selling. People loved the idea at the Surf Expo. We landed 30 accounts and by the summer, we had 150 accounts and sold out our entire inventory. I learned a valuable business lesson when I found out it took 90 days to get another order. I realized that SwitchFlops was no longer an experiment; it was a real business. I couldn't sell out of shoes again. More important, I needed an expert to help me run the business.

In January 2008, we hired Jeffery Davidson as our president and CEO. He has been nothing short of incredible. In 2007 we recorded approximately $700,000 in sales. In 2008, sales were $9 million. Last year, our sales hit $19 million. This year, our company is on pace to sell 1 million pairs of shoes and 2 million straps. Our projected revenue goal is $30 million. And to think, it all came from an idea born in a high school art class.

When I look back on this incredible adventure, I realize how lucky I've been to have good people around me and enough persistence and determination not to let the delays and setbacks keep me from making my dream a reality. Along the way, I've learned five important lessons that every new business owner should follow. They are:

Love What You Do and Work Hard at It. In order to be successful, you are going to have to work long hours and deal with a lot of ups and downs.

Ask for Help Along the Way. The worst thing that can happen is that people say "no!" If I didn't share my idea and ask for help, I never would have found a manufacturer.

Keep Your Head Up. People will say no to you. They will close doors in your face. Don't be discouraged. Keep moving forward with your idea. Believe in it and be persistent. Eventually, doors will open.

Hire the Right Team. Don't be afraid to bring people on board who are smarter than you. Success is rarely achieved alone. Take the time to build an incredible team.

In Life, Timing Is Key. When your moon and stars align, take your chance, run with it and have fun along the way.

CHAPTER 23

Building Merck's Future through Open Innovation

By Mervyn Turner, chief strategy officer at Merck

Mervyn Turner

Dr. Mervyn Turner spoke at the Rothman Institute's Third Annual Innovation Summit on April 30, 2008. At the time he was the senior vice president, worldwide licensing and external research at Merck Research Laboratories. He joined Merck in 1985 and since then has held many positions of increasing responsibility. In August 1999, he was appointed senior vice president of Merck Frosst Centre for Therapeutic Research in Montreal, Canada.

Turner returned from his assignment in Montreal in October 2002 to take responsibility for oversight of Merck's licensing activities and for management of academic relations. Through his diverse experiences in the Merck Research Laboratories, he has acquired a broad perspective on the issues surrounding drug discovery and development.

From 2004 to 2007 there was a sizeable increase in deal activity for Merck, with over 190 transactions completed. Merck has also been active in M&A, with Aton, Abmaxis, GlycoFi, Sirna and NovaCardia, all acquired to build areas of key strategic importance.

As of spring 2010, Turner holds the position of chief strategy officer at Merck and senior vice president of emerging markets research and development.

These are pretty tough times for the pharmaceutical sector as a whole. In reviewing our options, I see only one path for our company moving forward. We need to leverage open innovation on a worldwide basis.

Merck has a long history of innovation, but much of it has occurred internally. The challenge for our executive team has been to change Merck from an inwardly looking to an outward focused organization; a transformational shift for our company. The shift includes changes in our culture and mindset. To date, I believe we have been successful in incorporating these changes, and we are starting to see the results building.

Even though we had a reputation for being an inwardly focused organization, Merck has long been successful at licensing, going back to the time we licensed famotidine to get us into the H2 blocker market. PEPCID went on to be a very successful drug. Also most of our vaccines have required licenses to enable their development and commercialization.

We've also leveraged innovation through successful joint ventures. Astra and Merck formed a joint venture which gave us PRILOSEC, the world's number one selling drug. We have a joint venture with Johnson & Johnson which switched famotidine into a very successful over-the-coutner product. We had a very successful JV ("Merial") in Animal Health with sanofi-aventis, which we are currently looking to reconstitute post the Merck/Schering-Plough merger. We also had the Merck-Schering Plough alliances in both cardiovascular and respiratory medicine. These alliances have been very important to our business.

In 2000, we saw the industry landscape changing. Merck needed to focus much more rigorously on licensing. We had a number of patent expirations on big products coming up; there were gaps in our pipeline and we were dealing with several late stage development failures.

Although Merck had a successful history of partnering, we weren't really "out there." Other companies felt we suffered from "Not Invented Here (NIH) syndrome." At the time, Merck's goal was to license in one clinical development stage molecule each year, while other pharmaceutical companies were setting the pace with multiple partnerships. Back then, competition for deals was much less intense. In most cases, there were three or fewer companies involved in the licensing discussions. It was rare to have four or five companies participating, and never did we see five to eight companies in discussion. Well, those days are over.

Today, licensing discussions, in an environment where true innovation is a scarce resource, have become an auction process. As many as eight players can be involved in discussions with our potential partners. We asked ourselves, how can Merck distinguish itself in that kind of setting?

In 1988, we put together a straight-forward licensing agreement with Gentili, a small Italian company, to access alendronate, which became a very important drug called FOSAMAX, a successful treatment for osteoporosis. The deal included a small, up front royalty payment with no downstream participation by Gentili.

Today, companies demand, sometimes successfully, co-promotion rights in certain markets, sole marketing rights in their home market, and a voice in the development and commercialization process. We have tremendous debates and discussions with potential partners around reversion rights. What happens if this drug fails? And how we handle the intellectual property rights has become much more complicated to negotiate.

In this environment Merck needed to evolve into an outward facing organization. It was a very big transformation for us, one that required a strong message from the top. We weren't just talking about a change in Merck Research Labs, but closer ties with our partners in Corporate Licensing and Business Development, and our colleagues in Global Human Health (Sales and Marketing) as well. We were asking our people to make a big cultural shift to embrace partnering with outside organizations. In the process of changing the decision making mode, we found that our partners really didn't know how decisions got made at our company. Indeed, inside Merck, the process was considered opaque as well. That had to change.

The shift towards partnering started with understanding and re-engineering our processes from end to end. We looked at the entire landscape, and did internal and external benchmarking. We saw that our people needed to be better trained in how to deal with potential partners. We focused on the bottom line – how would we know if we were successful? To do that, we established a set of metrics to show how the changes were making a difference. Additionally, we worked hard to make our potential partners feel confident that Merck would be a great partner in helping to bring their products to market.

So we reworked our processes. We developed an overall licensing strategy aligned with the overall goals of Merck & Co. Inc. We worked on our people, our information systems, and we made sure that Merck's "Plan to Win" included acknowledgement of the need for partnerships. Importantly, we realigned our incentives so that whether an innovative solution comes from internal efforts or through external relationships, scientists involved in the identification of a drug will be rewarded.

The entire strategy was fully endorsed by the top management at

Merck. Dick Clark, our current CEO, travels several times a year to meet with potential partners. He also offers an open invitation to those partners to visit our headquarters. For those who have taken him up on the offer, Dick has always made time to meet and discuss our mutual interests.

Every year, Merck has more than 5,000 interactions with external parties. From these interactions, we typically generate about 50 deals a year. Our goal for each one is to leverage our internal capabilities through external collaborations. In doing so, we have tried to create a transparent and straightforward process which highlights the best ideas and capabilities of each partner. We continually evaluate potential transactions, which range from platform technologies to late stage product opportunities. All of this is highly coordinated across the entire company.

The process gives our employees and potential partners access to key decision makers throughout Merck, and consists of three elements: *opportunity identification*, *deal execution* and *alliance management*. A feature that we like about our approach is that our teams are not just centrally located at headquarters, but are distributed across different functions, at different research sites, and around the world wherever innovation might arise. Thus, senior level Merck scientists "on location" in biotech hubs like Boston and San Diego, our "scouts," aren't responsible for putting together deals. Instead, they build relationships in their local communities with academics, venture capitalists and biotech companies. The scouts are in these different geographical locations to interact with the biotech community because these companies are centers of innovation in our business. We need to be where they live and work. Building these types of long-term relationships has become a company wide activity for Merck. There is no stone left unturned when evaluating new opportunities. Our mantra is, "Ideas

Know No Boundaries".

As a company, Merck has embraced the mindset of going out to find innovation wherever it resides. Whether through arranging receptions at high profile events such as the American Heart Association meetings, or with private meetings with key potential partners or through high-level presentations at conferences around the world, Merck is never resting on its laurels. Instead, we are prospecting, building relationships and looking to get deals done. We have set up guiding principles to look at transactions in all stages of research and development. Merck is now fast, flexible, and focused on creating value and leveraging the strengths of each partner in our long-term relationships.

Today, Merck has a clear and straight-forward process which puts the company in a place to win in the battle for external opportunities. We have a system which prizes collaboration, and provides rapid access and involvement of senior management. We set objectives and continuously prioritize. We are an outwardly-focused, customer-driven company.

"Ideas Know No Boundaries!"

CHAPTER 24

The Eight Golden Rules of Entrepreneurship

By Peter Weedfald, president of Gen One Ventures,
and former chief marketing officer at Circuit City

Peter Weedfald

Peter Weedfald, BS '76, gave the keynote speech at the Rothman Institute's Sixth Annual Recognition Reception on September 7, 2007. At the time Weedfald was the chief marketing officer at Circuit City. Before joining Circuit City in 2006, he held senior positions at Samsung Electronics America.

Weedfald has also held senior positions with ViewSonic Corporation, a worldwide provider of advanced display technology, from 1998 to 2000. Weedfald served for nine years in executive publisher positions at Ziff-Davis Publishing, a leading integrated and on-line media company serving the technology and video game markets.

As of spring 2010, Weedfald is president of Gen One Ventures, where he collaborates with GE Licensing, providing sales, marketing, operations and retail channel consulting insights along with executive operational leadership for the various GE license partners.

I stand very honored to be here tonight, not because I am an oracle, autocrat, viceroy, or any of those other things. I am here tonight because my brothers and sisters asked me to come here tonight, and because I graduated from Fairleigh Dickinson University in 1976. And I have been honored to use the educational instruments that I received, from instructors who showed me the right way, and I have worked very hard as an entrepreneur in business.

I am going to give you the eight golden rules of entrepreneurship, in my humble opinion.

The first rule is on business judgment. You must have empirical business judgment 24 hours a day to be an entrepreneur. Business judgment is based on your ability to judge the one situation, one offer and one opportunity. It is a chance for you to park your ego at the door and make lucid decisions based on the facts, not on emotions.

The second rule of great entrepreneurship is on critical thinking. You must possess the power of critical thinking, to be able to stare down the cold steel of a profit and loss statement. If you think you can do this — prove it to yourself, prove that you are correct. Be a subject-matter expert, and use the power of critical thinking to make life decisions that will give you the will, the means and the need to be successful.

The third rule, in my humble opinion, is on sales motivation. In the language of salesmanship, I am a triple black belt. I studied, I got my face kicked in and my teeth ripped out. I went to church in between sales calls to pray to God for strength to close a deal. I got my butt kicked and I am proud of it. If you are not motivated to sell, then you are not going to make it as an entrepreneur. Selling is what I call the *fire in the belly*. For those of you who have the fire in the belly, you know you can't rent the fire in the belly, you can't lease it and you can't fake it. You can't take the blood out of another person who has the fire and put it in your veins. You either have it or you don't.

The fourth rule focuses on sales comprehension. It's not good enough to be motivated to sell. You must comprehend how to move the chess pieces around, offense and defense. You must know the best ways to stand, deliver and explain the value of your product to your potential clients or customers.

Rule five invokes the wisdom of Albert Einstein. I have a picture of him hanging in my office with the following quote: *"Creativity and imagination are more important than knowledge."* You have got to be creative in a way that is relevant to the market you serve. If you are not creative and you don't deploy imagination, you can never walk through the door of reasonable doubt, or the door of kinetic, torrid opportunity.

The sixth rule is an easy one. Give back. The spirit of generosity must be part of every great entrepreneur. Do something in your own community, where you grew up or in your church or synagogue. I was in New York City on 9/11. I was 10 blocks away from Ground Zero and lived through it. I decided to quit my job and went home. I realized then that I didn't see my wife enough or my child because I was sacrificing my blood to drive businesses for people in the spirit of entrepreneurship. After 9/11 I created a philanthropic program called Samsung's Four Seasons of Hope. The program is built around the Arnold Palmer Children's Hospital, the Magic Johnson Foundation, the Boomer Esiason Foundation, Jon Bon Jovi's Charities, The Guardian Angels and Joe Torre's Safe at Home Foundation. I continue to be very active in other charities for our wonderful children. We are blessed to have raised over 10 million dollars for the children of various causes, in seven short years.

Rule seven is harnessing and commanding the power of rejection.

In 1986, *Harvard Business Review* wrote an article about salesmen and why some salesmen fail. Entrepreneurship, to me, is all about selling an idea or concept to somebody and then following through. The article stated that almost 90% of all salespeople fail in their first year because they can't handle rejection. Today, "rejection" is a word that sounds like it came from the 1940's. No child goes without a color TV, iPod, PC and other devices. Today, we must teach people how to handle rejection.

The eighth golden rule is that questions are the answers. You control the power of being an entrepreneur by controlling the power of the question. My good friend who is an attorney will tell you that is what lawyers do. Doctors do it too. Remember this rule on the next visit to your physician. Tell him or her that you have a pain. The doctor will ask you, "Where is the pain?" You reply, "It's right here." They will ask you how you got the pain, when it hurts and if you think pain medication might help to relieve your problem. You answer their questions, and the next thing you know, they're handing you a bill for $122 and telling you to see the nurse.

To sum up the eight golden rules--you have to know your market and your potential buyers. You must understand the strengths and weaknesses of your competition. You need Key Performance Indexes (KPI's). You need to have a P&L statement that shows gross margin in profit and revenue. The business plan is incomplete if you can't explain how you plan to get from here to there and whether or not you are going to make money.

If you understand the spirit of generosity and giving to others, and you understand the importance of the P&L and the business plan, then you are well on your way to becoming a great entrepreneur.

ABOUT THE EDITOR

James Barrood is the Executive Director of the nationally recognized Rothman Institute of Entrepreneurship at Fairleigh Dickinson University's Silberman College of Business. He has developed and managed many of the Institute's innovative academic and outreach programs since 1997. Barrood has won several honors, is frequently quoted in print and online media and often appears as a guest on TV programs to discuss entrepreneurship and innovation.

CPSIA information can be obtained at www.ICGtesting.com
Printed in the USA
LVOW100201020612

284324LV00004B/54/P